enjoying
SKATING

enjoying
SKATING

by the Diagram Group

PADDINGTON PRESS LTD
NEW YORK & LONDON

Library of Congress Cataloging in Publication Data
Diagram Group
   Enjoying skating
   Includes index.
    1. Skating.   2. Roller-skating.   3. Skateboarding.
   1. Title.
   GV849.D5   796.2'1   78-9152
   ISBN 0 7092 0138 9
   ISBN 0 448 22194 2 (U.S. and Canada only)

Printed and bound in Scotland by Morrison & Gibb Ltd., Edinburgh
Diagram Visual Information Ltd
Editor Eleanor Van Zandt
Art Editor Diana C. Taylor
Artists Nigel Bailey, Andrew Chapman, Stephen Clark, Sarah Fox-Davies,
Sheila Galbraith, Robert Galvin, Brian Hewson, Richard Hummerstone,
David Lightfoot, János Márffy, Kathleen McDougall, Graham Rosewarne,
Consultants Colin Forrest, National Skating Association of Great Britain,
Sports-Drome Ltd. U.K.
Picture Researcher Linda Proud
Picture Credits All-Sport - Tony Duffy   Page 29"The Skater"(1051)
The Mansell Collection   Gilbert Stuart
Camera Press   National Gallery of Art,
Mike Benson   Washington DC
Mrs Ed Lacey   Andrew W. Mellon collection
Interaction

In the United States PADDINGTON PRESS
Distributed by
Grosset & Dunlap
In the United Kingdom PADDINGTON PRESS
In Canada Distributed by
RANDOM HOUSE OF CANADA LTD.
In Southern Africa Distributed by
ERNEST STANTON (PUBLISHERS) (PTY.) LTD.

Foreword

Enjoying Skating introduces the world of skating in its exciting and varied entirety — from the time it was just a means of getting from place to place in frozen climates to its development into several magnificent sports, all combining the elements of precision, speed, grace and athletic skill. Whether you're interested in figure skating, where the skaters execute movements of lyrical beauty, or in ice hockey, where players encased in padding zoom over the ice and converge on each other like human billiard balls, there's something here for you.

First, there's an introductory chapter showing basic ice skating techniques. Next is a detailed section on figure skating. The third chapter looks at the skills involved in artistic roller skating, and the fourth covers the exhilarating sport of speed skating in its various forms. A chapter on the fast and furious game of hockey comes next, and the final chapter explains the basic skills and some of the daring maneuvers involved in skateboarding.

In order to become a skilled skater, you'll need a teacher or coach. This is particularly true in learning the more advanced movements, such as jumps. But before you get to this stage, *Enjoying Skating,* with its easy-to-read text and wealth of step-by-step illustrations, will equip you with a solid understanding of many of the basic skills that make skating so enjoyable for participants and spectators alike.

Our special thanks go to the coaches who have lent their expertise to the creation of this book. We hope that it will encourage more people, young and old, to discover for themselves the pleasures of skating in all its many forms.

Contents

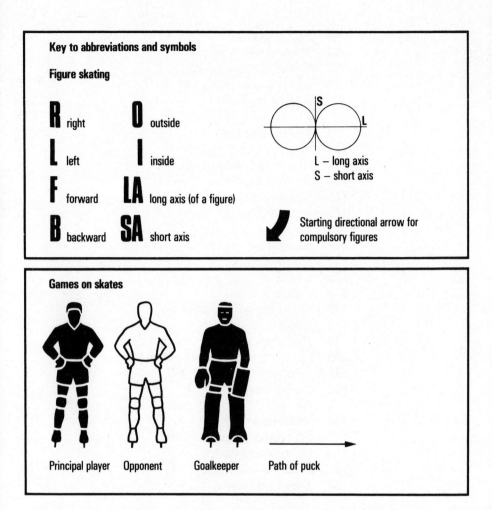

Key to abbreviations and symbols

Figure skating

R right   **O** outside

L left   **I** inside

F forward   **LA** long axis (of a figure)

B backward   **SA** short axis

L – long axis
S – short axis

Starting directional arrow for compulsory figures

Games on skates

Principal player   Opponent   Goalkeeper   Path of puck

"Motorskates" are the latest of many skating innovations.

Introduction

Skaters photographed around the turn of the century practice their sport in the open air.

Today, people skate for fun. But the earliest skaters probably regarded their skates as a means of transport. Bone runners dating back to New Stone Age times have been discovered in northern Europe. They may have been used by migrating tribes in order to cross frozen lakes and rivers. Scandinavian sagas of around 1200 refer to the skating ability of certain gods and heroes, indicating that skill on the ice was greatly admired.

In the Middle Ages a chronicler of life in London described how people amused themselves on the ice: ". . . some tie bones to their feet, and under their heels, and shoving themselves by a little picked staff, do slide as swiftly as a bird flyeth in the air, or an arrow out of a crossbow . . . ."

A 15th-century Dutch woodcut shows a young girl who has fallen on the ice being helped up by her companions. The girl, whose name was Liedwi, never completely recovered from her fall and spent the rest of her life in a religious order. She is considered the patron saint of skaters.

The print illustrating St. Liedwi's accident shows people wearing bladed skates, which would have been made of iron. This kind of skate was probably developed in the Netherlands, where the network of canals made skating the natural way of getting from one place to another during the winter. The Dutch became expert skaters. Once, during their wars with the Spanish, they foiled an attempt to capture their ice-bound ships by fighting the Spaniards on skates.

Battles on skates are a thing of the past — unless you count ice hockey, a fast and ferocious game especially popular in North America. From its utilitarian origins, skating has developed along several different lines — figure skating, speed skating, and skating games. All of these can be done on rollers as well as blades. Recently a new sport — skateboarding — has burst on the scene. Skating has come a long way from sliding across the ice on two strips of bone.

Ice-skating Victorian style in London's Kensington Gardens.

When you first begin to ice skate it's a good idea to rent your skates. Most rinks have a shop where skates can be rented. Then once you're sure you want to continue skating you should buy the best boots and skates you can afford and have the blades fitted to the boots by an expert. From time to time your skates will need to be sharpened; this, too, should be done by a skilled person.

It is most important for the skating boot to fit snugly. However, there should be enough room in the boot to accommodate a pair of woolen socks. The boots should be leather-lined and the arches firmly reinforced.
The sole should be about $^3/_{10}$ in (8mm) thick so that strong screws may be used in attaching the skates. All figure skates have blades that are concave on the bottom so that they have two sharp edges. They also have a jagged toe, called a toe rake, or pick, used in some stops and also in jumps and spins. There are figure skates designed specially for doing the compulsory figures, for free skating, and for ice dancing. To begin with, choose a general-purpose blade and make sure it is about the length of the boot – or slightly longer if your feet are still growing and you'll be needing larger boots.
The blade should be attached to the boot so that it passes along the line between the big toe and the second toe and centrally under the heel. It is possible to attach some skates temporarily so that you can check the balance before they are screwed on permanently.

For skating outdoors you'll need warm clothing, of course. Slacks (not too tight-fitting) and a warm sweater are appropriate for both boys and girls. For indoor rinks, choose lighter-weight clothing, but keep a cardigan handy for rest periods. Girls may prefer to wear a skirt instead of slacks, along with opaque tights, which will keep your legs warmer than sheer pantyhose and will last much longer. A pair of gloves is useful when you've fallen down and need to push yourself up off the ice.

Once you've discovered that you enjoy skating, you may want to get special clothes for it. Girls usually find that a short skating skirt gives the legs more freedom of movement, as well as looking graceful. Boys can get pants made of stretch fabric, which allows the flexibility needed particularly in free skating.

Skate guards are essential for protecting the blades when you step off the ice. When you get home, remove the guards and dry the blades thoroughly with a soft cloth to prevent rust. Keep your boots in good condition with colorless shoe cream.

Your first attempts to skate will make you feel like a character in a slapstick movie. Your normally cooperative legs will slide this way and that, ignoring your wishes. The natural tendency is to try to walk across the ice. But nearly all skating is done on one foot at a time, so you must learn to balance on one foot and glide — not walk — over the ice.

What enables you to glide is that the pressure of the skate and the weight of the skater cause friction, which in turn generates heat, melting the ice ever so slightly. The moisture makes the ice slippery. As the skate passes over the ice, the moisture re-freezes behind it, but so rapidly that the track of the skate remains etched on it.

The two edges of a figure skate make it possible to skate in a curved line. As a beginner, however, you'll skate on the flat of the blade — that is, on the two edges at the same time.

 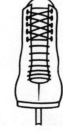 

Angling the body to the right or the left will turn the skate on an edge, producing movement in a curved line.

Your skates are curved upward slightly at the front and the back to facilitate turns. Most of the time your weight should be balanced over the center of the blade. When you're skating forward the weight should be slightly to the rear of the center point; when skating backward, slightly to the front of it.

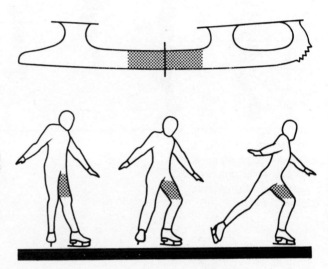

One reason beginners lose their balance is that they keep their knees stiff. Remember to bend your knees and balance your weight on the thigh of the skating leg. The thigh muscles do most of the work in skating. Concentrate on controlling the thigh muscles, and this control will naturally extend to your feet.

Instinctively, you will use your arms for balance. Normally, to begin with, you should hold them slightly out from the body, about waist-high, with the palms down. When you start to do curves you'll need to learn to move your arms in the opposite way to the way you move them when walking. Whereas in walking the arms and legs swing forward in opposition, in skating they often move together — for example, left arm and leg forward, right arm and leg back. This may seem awkward at first, but once mastered, it looks very graceful.

Before going out onto the ice, make sure your boots are laced correctly. They should be tightly laced at the ankles and more loosely at the top.

Begin by getting the feel of the ice. Holding onto the bar, practice shifting your weight from one foot to the other. Lift one foot, then the other, off the ice. Practice this without holding onto the bar. Next, try some deep knee bends. Hold your arms out in front and bend your knees until you're in a squatting position. Keep your back as straight as possible, though leaning forward.

Learning to fall correctly is important. When you begin to fall try to sit down. You're less likely to hurt yourself if you land on your bottom. Keep your hands up – don't try to stop the fall. As you start to slip, bend your knees so that you won't fall so far. To get up, first roll over into a kneeling position. Place your hands on the ice, about 12in (30cm) apart. Bring one foot forward about even with the other knee. Then bring the other foot forward. Lift your hands up and out in front of you so that you're balanced on your feet. Then, keeping your arms forward, rise to a standing position. It's a good idea to practice falling on purpose and getting up so that you'll know what to do when you fall accidentally.

Your first steps on the ice will be short ones. Start with your feet in a "T" position, the right behind the left. Push backward with the right foot, using the full length of the blade, not just the toe. At the same time, shift the weight to the left foot and glide forward at a slight angle. Keep the right foot stretched out behind you, toe pointed outward, and the knee of the left foot bent. When you start to run out of speed, bring the right foot up to the left foot. Shift your weight onto the right foot and push back with the left foot, as before.

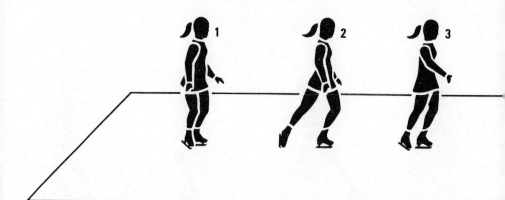

Once you can skate forward in short strokes you should learn to skate in long gliding steps.

1 begin as before with a push backward on the right foot.
2 glide forward on the left.

3 gradually straighten the left leg and at the same time bring the right leg up to it.

Most beginning skaters come to a stop by heading for the rail and grabbing it. Here are some better ways of stopping when you're skating forward.

half snowplow
Glide forward on both feet, with the feet a few inches apart. Then push one foot out to the side, keeping the blade flat. Your forward movement will cause it to angle inward and act as a brake.

4 bend the left leg again, shifting the weight slightly to the right. This will make you turn slightly to the right.

5 shift the weight onto the right leg and thrust back with the left.
6 straighten up as in fig. 3.

7 bend again as in fig. 4, and continue as before. Each glide will be at a slight angle to the previous one.

snowplow
Glide forward as for the half snowplow, then force both heels outward and bring the knees together.

hockey
Glide forward on both feet; bend the knees; then straighten up, at the same time turning both feet to the left; then bend knees again and twist the body to the right. (The stop can also be done in the opposite direction.)

T-stop
Glide forward on one foot with the other stretched out behind. Gradually lower the free foot onto the ice behind the skating foot, making a 90° angle to it, with the blade on the outside edge. It will brake you slowly to a stop.

First practice at the bar, holding on with one hand and lifting one foot then the other. Move the skating foot backward a few inches, then shift to the other foot and glide backward a few inches on it. When you have practiced making these short backward steps, go out onto the ice and practice making long backward glides.

A competitor demonstrates the kind of balance to aim for.

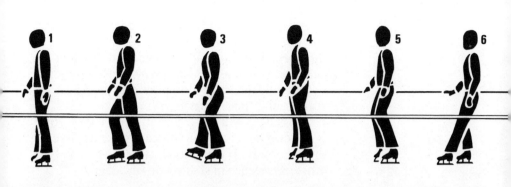

1 begin by standing with your toes a little apart and pointing slightly inward. Your weight should be balanced on both feet.
2 bend both knees and push the left foot back diagonally, at the same time pushing forward on the inside edge of the right foot.

3 looking backward over the left shoulder, and keeping the knees well bent, glide backward on the left foot with the right foot held forward.

4 slowly straighten the left knee and bring the right foot close to the left.

5 shift the weight to the right foot, at the same time bending the knees, and turn the head to the right.

6 glide backward on the right foot and continue as before.

To make a backward stop, you use the toe pick of your skate. Practice these two stops first at a slow speed and then while skating faster.

single toe scratch
While gliding backward on both feet, move one foot to the rear and lift the heel off the ice. The toe pick will then brake you to a stop. The body should be leaning slightly forward if you are skating slowly; farther forward if you are skating fast.

double toe scratch
While gliding backward on both feet, raise both heels and lean forward. The toe picks will brake you to a stop.

One of the first problems the beginning skater encounters is how to get around the corners of the rink. Stopping at the end and starting up again at a 90° angle isn't very satisfactory. So you should learn to do some crossovers to get you around those corners.

Crossovers will get you skating on edges, for it is only on an edge that you can make a curve on the ice. Next, try a chassé, which will give you more experience in skating on one edge.

Practice getting the feel of crossovers while standing at the bar. Raise the right foot and bring it around in front of the left so that the right heel is beside the left toe. Then lift the left foot, toe first, and bring it around beside the right foot as before. Practice this until it feels natural.

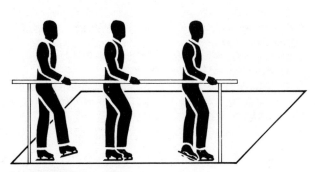

forward chassé
1 thrust off with the right foot and glide forward on the left outside edge. The left knee should be bent at the start, then straightened, and the right leg should be stretched out behind and to the side.
2 bring the right foot forward parallel to the left and place it on the ice for a moment, with both knees bent.
3 thrust off again with right foot and continue on left forward outside edge.

left forward crossover

1 thrust off onto the left foot and shift weight to outside edge, keeping the knee well bent and the right leg stretched out diagonally behind.

2 bring the right leg forward and place it on the ice on the inside edge beside the left foot. The right toe should point slightly to the left, and the knee should be bent.

3 shift weight to right inside edge and stretch left leg out behind and slightly outside the circle.

4 bring left leg up beside right leg and thrust off onto left foot, right leg behind. Continue this sequence of movements, which will take you in a curve around to the left. For right crossovers, reverse these directions.

4 bring the feet together again as in step 2, but also bring the right hip forward slightly and shift the weight to the right foot.

5 thrust off with the left foot and glide forward on the right.

6 and **7** continue, as in steps 2 and 3, reversing directions.

Figure skating

Pair skaters performing the spectacular "death spiral"

Although skating in some form has been practiced for many hundreds of years, the art of making graceful shapes on the ice developed only since the early 18th century. The potential for figure skating already existed in the "Dutch roll"—skating on one outside edge then the other—which made it possible to skate in a curved line. In England, where skating was usually on ponds, rather than on canals as in the Netherlands, distance skating soon gave way to skating in circles, and it was in this country that the first figure skate was made. The first book on skating, published in England in 1772, described a number of figures and free skating movements including spirals, the curve eight and the forward three.

In the 19th century, while the English concentrated on devising more intricate figures, performed in a restrained and often rather stiff manner, skaters on the Continent and in America were developing a freer style characterized by graceful dancelike movements. The Viennese style, which was inspired mainly by the flamboyant American skater Jackson Haines, dominated international skating from the mid-1800s onward and was finally adopted by the English around the turn of the century.

The discipline of the English style remains in the compulsory figures that every amateur competitor must be able to do. In this century a new element has been added: acrobatics. The spectacular leaps and spins with which innovators such as Sonja Henie and Dick Button dazzled audiences are now part of any top skater's repertoire. Modern figure skating is a blend of precision, grace and vigorous athletics — an art and a sport in one.

If you want to participate in competitions you must belong to a skating club. The clubs in each country are grouped into national associations; which in turn are members of the International Skating Union. The ISU decides all organizational and technical questions.

A detail from "The Skater" by the American painter Gilbert Stuart illustrates the sedate style popular in the 18th and 19th centuries.

Circles and figures

Once you can skate forward and backward on all four edges you should learn how to trace a circle on the ice. The correct thrust-off is most important, but you must also, while making the circle, coordinate the movements of legs, arms, torso and head very subtly in order to make the circle symmetrical.

On the following pages are instructions for performing a few of the 41 compulsory, or "school," figures that every competitor must be able to do.

thrusting off—RFO

1 begin at the intersection of the LA and SA with the R foot pointing forward and the L foot just behind pointing outward. The torso is facing forward.
2 bend the knees and push down and back on the LI edge, which will send you forward (this movement is sometimes called the strike); the first skate length traveled is on flat of blade.
3 lean toward the center of the circle, keeping R arm forward and L arm back, free foot pointed outward.
For LFO curves reverse these instructions.

thrusting off—RBO
This movement is more complicated than the forward thrust-off as it involves turning the body around.
1 stand at the intersection of the LA and SA with the toe of the L skate at the intersection and the R foot a short distance away pointing diagonally toward the SA; both skates should be flat on the ice and most of the weight on the L leg.

2 bend the L knee a bit more and simultaneously bring the L foot backward across the LA while moving the R foot around so that the toe is in front of the toe of the L foot.
3 move the R foot backward along the SA, shifting the weight to the R leg, and at the same time thrust with the inside edge of the L skate.

4 angle the body slightly to the right; keep R arm forward and L arm back and look over your R shoulder.
For LBO curves reverse these instructions.

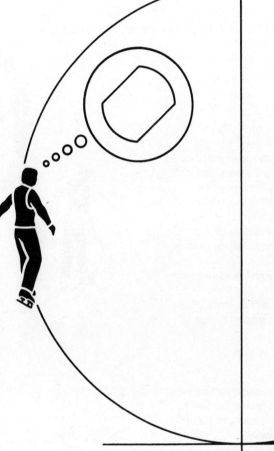

composing a circle

The circles that make up the compulsory figures are aligned on long and short axes: the long axis dividing each circle in half and the short axis running between each two circles. Each circle is begun at the intersection of the two axes. In learning to skate a perfect circle you may find it helpful first to trace the axes on the ice and perhaps also mark the quarter and three-quarter points.

Before beginning the circle follow its path with your eyes so that you know in advance where you want to go. Paradoxically, if you "think straight" during the second and fourth quarters of the circle these quarters will be round; whereas if you "think round," as for the first and third, they will tend to bulge outward.

This figure consists of two joined circles performed on the same edge of each foot — for example, the right forward outside for one circle and the left forward outside for the second.

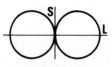

curve eight-RFO-LFO

1 thrust off as already described; after a quarter turn, knees should be almost straight.

2 just before halfway point bring free foot – still pointing outward – slightly ahead of tracing foot.

3 move free foot forward until heel is by toe of tracing foot just outside of line of tracing; at same time move R arm back slightly.

4 begin moving L arm toward the front.

5 by the three-quarters point the change of posture is completed.

6 begin changeover movement by bringing R arm well back and drawing L foot in parallel to tracing foot; bend knees and straighten inclination of body; just before reaching LA, turn tracing foot toward the center on the inner edge.

7 at LA push L foot forward on the SA.

The second circle, on the LFO, is the mirror image of the first.

curve eight-RBO-LBO

The instructions are for a figure in which the skater looks outside the circle. Another figure is the backward outside curve eight in which the skater looks into the circle.

1 thrust off on RBO as already described and shift weight to outside edge. In beginning the curve look inside the circle; turn hips slightly to the right; keep R arm forward, L arm out to side, free foot just ahead of tracing foot.

2 at quarter circle turn head to face outside.

3 at halfway point begin moving free foot past tracing foot, keeping toe turned out; begin shifting arm position.

4 at three-quarter point complete change of posture; free foot is now behind tracing foot and L arm is forward.

5 just before LA begin changeover; move free foot slightly farther back; keep weight on RO edge.

6 at LA bend knees and turn heel of tracing foot sharply into circle, bringing it up to R toe.

7 move L foot along SA and thrust off with inner edge of R foot, at the same time bending L knee deeply and shifting the weight to this foot.

The second circle, on the LBO, is the mirror image of the first.

Many of the figures and free skating movements involve a change from one edge to the other on the same foot or a change of direction on the same foot — for example, from forward outside to backward inside. This second kind of movement is called a three turn because the line traced on the ice curves inward and outward, as in the point of the numeral three.

First practice changing edge. This will be very useful when you try to make a curve eight on one foot.

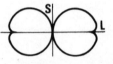

three turn—RFO—RBI

1 begin the curve on RFO, as for a curve eight.
2 about one-third of the way around the circle bring the R arm back and the L arm forward.
3 just before the LA bring the L arm across the body and the L foot farther back, and lean farther into the circle. Skate into the circle and "roll off" the front of the skate. This is done by rocking forward on the blade and immediately changing edge. The change— that is, the point of the three — should be exactly on the LA.
4 move back on the RBI onto the line of the circle by immediately reversing the arm position. Keep the free foot back. Complete the circle.

5 at LA turn the body into the circle, swing L arm in direction of travel, and bring R arm across body. Turn R heel into new circle.
6 thrust off on L foot with L arm forward and R arm back. Complete the figure with a LFO-LBI three turn.

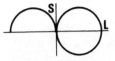

changes-RFO—RFI

1 begin a circle on RFO, bringing L foot and L arm forward.

2 about one-third of the way around the circle turn the hips to the left and bring R arm forward and L arm back.

3 just before LA swing the L foot farther forward and bring R arm across in front of the body, at the same time straightening R leg.

4 at LA change to RFI edge by shifting the weight into the new circle and bending the skating leg.

5 bring free foot to rear and move arms back to normal position. Complete the circle on RFI.

Practice this movement from LFO to LFI.

In this figure, instead of making one turn at the long axis, you make two turns, at one-third and two-thirds of the way around the circle. In other words, if you think of the starting point as 6 o'clock, your first three turn will be at 10 o'clock and the second at 2 o'clock. Positioning the turns accurately is tricky, but you'll find it helpful if when beginning the circle you look toward 9 o'clock. First practice making this single turn and completing the circle normally, then work on placing the second three turn.

1 thrust off on RFO, fixing line of sight at 9 o'clock.
2 at 9 o'clock turn hips to the right, swing R arm back, L arm forward, and lean in toward center of circle. Make a three turn as described on the previous page.
3 on moving back onto the line of the circle on RBI, glance toward the 2 o'clock position, then immediately look out of the circle. Arms should be in normal position and free foot back.
4 bring the R arm back and move the L arm and foot forward.
5 move L foot slightly across the curve and bring L arm in front of body. Make a three turn by skating into the circle and rolling off the skate with a rocking motion from the front part of the skate to the back, changing to the FO edge.
6 move back into the line of the circle, shifting R arm forward and L arm back, and moving free foot back. Complete the circle on RFO.
7 at LA, change to LFO and complete the figure with a LFO/LBI-LFO double three.

Young skaters learning to mark out circles for compulsory figures. Each circle should be 3 times the skater's height.

Loops are much smaller than the other figures. The diameter of the circle is about the same as the skater's height from shoulders to feet. Just before the long axis the skater moves into the circle and traces an egg-shaped curve, about one skate length wide and one-and-a-half lengths long. The figure is skated on the same edge, with a change to the same edge on the other foot at the intersection of the two axes.

loop—RFI
1 thrust off on RFI, keeping tracing leg deeply bent, free foot stretched out behind, R arm forward, L arm back. Concentrate on moving along the LA so as to restrict your outward movement and keep the circle small.

2 at about one-third of the way around the circle, lean heavily into the circle and move the free foot outside the curve of the circle.
3 move free foot farther to the side and press the knee into the back of the R knee.

4 skate into the circle, bringing R hip forward.

5 continue counterclockwise turn, bringing free leg forward, knee first, close to tracing leg.

6 with free leg extended forward, continue on the line of the circle, straightening tracing leg slightly.

7 move L arm forward and R arm back, and bring L foot back toward tracing foot, crossed slightly in front of it. Complete the circle.

A bracket is the opposite of a three turn. At the long axis, instead of skating into the circle, you skate out of it, then change edge and complete the circle.

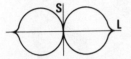

bracket – RFO – RBI/LBI – LFO
1 thrust off on RFO, with R arm forward and L arm slightly back. The L leg should be stretched out behind and slightly outside the circle. Look at the place on the LA where you will make the turn.
2 about one-quarter of the way around the circle, bring the L leg close to R leg and move arms farther forward and back so that the shoulders are in line with the tracing.

3 just before LA straighten the R knee. Then make the turn out of the circle, rolling off the front part of the skate and immediately shifting to the inside leg. At the point of the bracket there should be a tiny cross on the ice.
4 just after making the turn, bring L leg forward on a line with the tracing toe and bring the R arm forward and L arm back. Keep the tracing knee well bent.

5 at about three-quarters of the way around the circle reverse the arms, swing the free leg back, and look in toward the center of the circle.
6 just before the LA bring the feet together.
7 thrust off on LBI for the second half of the figure. Reverse directions of steps 1 and 2. Make the turn by skating outside of circle and rolling off back part of blade onto LFO edge. Complete the circle.

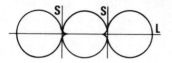

rocker (above)
The movement that gives this figure its name is a sharp outward turn on one foot from a forward to a backward direction, or vice versa. The instructions that follow are for a rocker done on the outside edges.
1 begin with a semicircle on the RFO, free arm forward.
2 approaching LA bring free arm farther forward and tracing arm back; move free foot forward.
3 at LA shoulders should be parallel with tracing. Raise free foot, straighten tracing knee and turn clockwise onto RBO, at same time bending tracing knee.

4 complete the circle on RBO.
5 at LA change to LBO edge and skate a semicircle, bringing free arm and leg back around halfway point.
6 approaching LA bring free arm and leg farther back and move tracing arm across the body.
7 at LA shoulders should be parallel with tracing. Straighten tracing knee and bring free foot back toward tracing foot, at the same time turning clockwise onto LFO. Complete the circle.

counter (below)
Like the rocker, the counter involves a turn from forward to backward, or vice versa, but the turn is made inward, rather than outward.

1 begin with a semicircle on the RFI. Around halfway point move free arm and leg forward.

2 just before LA move free arm farther forward and tracing arm back so that shoulders are parallel with tracing. Lean slightly into circle to be skated.

3 at LA straighten the tracing knee and turn clockwise onto the RBI. The turn should be made on the front part of the skate. Immediately after the turn move the free leg forward in line with the tracing foot. Complete the circle on RBI.

4 at LA change to LBI edge and skate a semicircle. Around halfway point move free arm and leg backward.

5 approaching LA move free arm farther back and tracing arm forward so that shoulders are parallel with tracing.

6 at LA straighten the tracing knee and bring the free leg back toward the tracing leg. Make a clockwise turn, on the front part of the skate, onto the LFI edge. Complete the circle on the LFI.

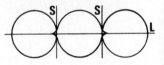

Change double threes

This figure is based on the three turns you've already learned, but it involves changes of edge at the long axis. Instructions are for changes on forward edges, but the figure may also be done starting on a backward edge.

1 skate a semicircle on RFO, beginning with free foot and arm forward, R arm back.

2 approaching LA bring R arm forward and L arm back, and move free foot farther forward.

3 at LA shift weight into the new circle to change to RFI.

4 immediately after change, move free foot back and free arm forward. Look at the place on the ice where you will make the first three turn.

5 at the "3 o'clock" point on the circle begin to draw R arm in front of body and move L arm farther back.

6 lean farther into the circle and roll off the front of the skate onto the RBO. Immediately bring L arm back and look outside the circle.

7 after passing LA bring R arm farther forward. Just before point of second three, pull L arm sharply to rear and bring R arm in front of body. Make second three by rolling off back of skate onto RFI edge.

8 immediately rotate arms so that L arm is across body, R arm behind, and bring free foot forward.

9 at LA thrust off with R foot onto LFI and skate a semicircle, gradually bringing free foot forward. Just before LA bring L arm well back and R arm forward.

10 shift weight into new circle and onto LFO and immediately bring free foot back.

Complete the figure with a double three onto LBI and then onto LFO.

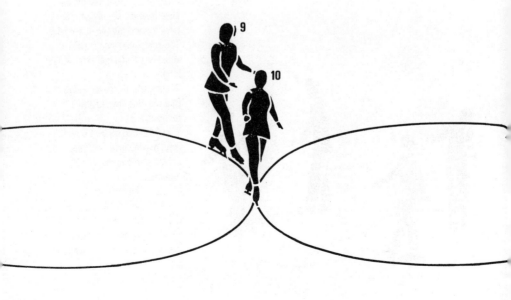

Here is another figure involving changes of edge. Remember that the loop is a small figure — the diameter of the circles being approximately the same as the height of the skater.

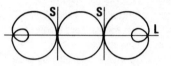

change loop–RFO–RFI/LFI–LFO

1 skate a semicircle on RFO, taking the free arm and leg forward right away and looking at the place on the LA where you will make the change.

2 just at LA straighten the tracing knee and bring the tracing arm forward. Shift the weight into the new circle to change to RFI.

3 bring the free leg back, and at a point about one-third of the way around the circle take the free foot slightly outside the circle. Lean into the circle toward the bottom of the imagined loop.

4 at LA bring the tracing hip farther forward and skate into the circle.

5 at the half-way point of the loop, on LA, bring free hip and knee forward slightly and turn back toward the top of the loop. The completed loop should be about one-and-a-half skate lengths long.

6 complete the circle, keeping free foot and tracing arm forward.

7 at LA strike off on LFI and skate a semicircle, with the tracing arm and the free leg forward.

8 at LA take the free arm forward and bring the tracing arm slightly back. Take the free leg back quickly and shift the weight into the new circle to change to LFO.

9 keeping free leg back and slightly outside the circle and free arm well forward and tracing arm well back, begin circle for loop.

10 at one-third point lean heavily into circle and bring free foot around to side of tracing foot.

11 at LA turn slightly into the circle, continuing to bring free foot forward.

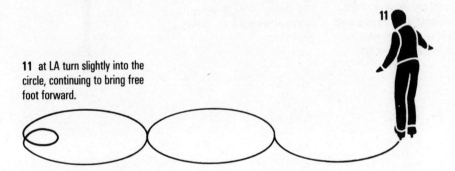

12 make the loop, gradually bringing free foot ahead of tracing foot and turning hips to the right. After completing the loop the free foot should be well forward, the tracing arm slightly forward, and the free arm to the side.

13 complete the circle, bringing free foot back toward skating foot, with toe pointed out.

A free skating program includes a variety of jumps, spins, spirals, turns, and dance steps linked in a sequence that expresses the mood and tempo of the music. Many free skating movements incorporate parts of the compulsory figures, such as rockers and counters — proof of the value of learning these figures even if you don't plan to compete. Jumps and spins demand plenty of practice before they can be performed with that "effortless" grace that is the essence of free skating.

spirals
The name of this movement derives from the fact that if you hold the position long enough you will trace a large spiral on the ice. Normally, a spiral is held for a relatively short time, but it makes a graceful and effective contrast to jumps and spins. To do a spiral skate forward on one edge and lift the free leg straight out behind you with the toe turned out. Keep your back well arched and your free leg straight. It's most important to keep your arms up — beginners have a tendency to let them drop. Another thing to remember is to keep the heel of the skating foot firmly on the ice in order to keep your balance.

spread-eagle
In this movement the toes are turned outward and the skater glides around in a circle on the outside or inside edges. To do an inside spread-eagle:
1 run forward to build up speed.
2 glide forward on RO edge.
3 bring free foot forward, toe pointing out, then back and onto the ice just in front of the R foot; at the same time bring R shoulder back sharply, and turn R foot onto inside edge.
4 shift body weight into the circle.

1

pivot
You can pivot either forward or backward. Start by learning the forward inside pivot in a counterclockwise direction.
1 skate forward on RI, making a small curve, with your L foot inside the circle and your free arm back and tracing arm forward.
2 place the L toe pick lightly on the ice and let it move along over the surface of the ice, while the R foot continues to trace an ever-decreasing circle.
3 when the circle becomes quite small, throw your weight onto the pivoting toe and move the R foot around it.

Choctaw

In essence this is a counter done on two feet. The instructions that follow are for a RFI-LBO closed Choctaw.

1 skate forward on RI edge keeping L foot just behind R foot, at a right angle to it; L arm forward, R arm to side.

2 turn into circle and shift weight to LBO.

3 continue on LBO, with R foot at toe of L foot, pointing outward; R arm back and L arm forward.

Mohawk

This movement is similar to a bracket but is done on two feet. The instructions that follow are for a LFO-RBO open Mohawk.

1 begin as for a LFO-LBI bracket, skating on the LFO with L shoulder and arm forward and R shoulder, arm and foot back, toe turned out.

2 approaching the apex of the bracket, swing the R leg, hip and shoulder forward.

3 at the apex, bend the R knee and bring R foot down just behind L foot on outside edge; swing L foot back and turn toe outward. For a closed Mohawk, after the turn keep free foot forward.

drop Mohawk

This is similar to the Mohawk already described, but the drop Mohawk itself is skated on inside edges, making a three on the ice, rather than a bracket, and the movement is completed with a step onto the BO edge.

1 approach on LFI with L arm to side, R arm forward and R foot back.

2 bring R foot up beside L foot and at a right angle to the L instep, at the same time turning shoulders clockwise.

3 as you turn, step onto the RBI and extend the L foot backward along the line of travel. Keep R arm and shoulder well forward, L arm and shoulder back.

4 immediately change to LBO, keeping arms and shoulders in same position.

5 complete the movement by moving R foot and arm back.

The jumps are the real crowd-pleasers, and every skater aspires to do them. Of course they are difficult. In order to achieve a good high jump you must first of all build up considerable speed. As you go into the jump you must bend the knee of the skating foot and thrust up strongly with the thigh muscles.

Most jumps involve rotating in the air. You will soon discover which direction of turn is more natural for you. For right-handed skaters it is usually the counterclockwise direction; for left-handed skaters, clockwise. Remember to lift your arms on take-off to help gain height, to draw them in toward the body to assist the rotation, and to open them on landing to check the rotation.

Salchow

1 begin preparation on LBI.
2 change to RFO and make a three turn.
3 skate backward on RBI with L foot stretched out behind; bend R knee.
4 swing the L foot to the side then to front of the tracing foot.
5 take off as the free foot crosses the line of the tracing foot; move the free foot upward and thrust up from the pick of the R skate.
6 make one complete rotation.
7 land on the LBO edge, R foot and arm forward, L arm to side.
8 swing R leg backward and sideways; rotate arms.
The Salchow (pronounced *sal*-co") may also be done from LBI to RBO.

three jump

This is sometimes called a waltz jump. It consists of a half rotation in the air so that when you land you are facing in the direction from which you started.

1 begin the preparation by skating on the LBO edge.

2 make a quarter turn onto the RFO edge; keep the skating leg bent and the free leg stretched out behind; R arm forward, L arm back.

3 for the take-off swing both arms up and forward; swing the L foot sideways and upward and at the same time thrust upward with the R leg.

4 during the turn, at the highest point of the jump, the body should be perpendicular to the ice.

5 land on LBO, R arm forward, L arm well back; free foot is forward on landing; bring it immediately to the rear and sideways with the toe turned out.

The three jump may also be done from LFO to RBO.

Axel (below)
This jump, often performed in competitions, involves rotating one-and-a-half times in the air. A variation, called the inside Axel, has one turn.
1 after making a three turn from LBI to LFO, approach jump on LFO, keeping knees well bent.
2 at take-off shoulders should face ahead almost squarely; lift R leg forward and upward sharply; push off from L toe.

3 make one-and-a-half rotations keeping arms close in toward the body.
4 land on RBO and immediately bring L foot backward.
The Axel may also be done from RFO to LBO.

Lutz jump (left)

1 run into the jump on the RBO, starting with the L foot held close to the tracing foot and pointing downward slightly.
2 move free foot to the rear and bend R knee; R arm should be well forward and L arm back.

3 pick into ice with L toe about 6-10 in (15-25cm) to the right of the skating line; drop arms and keep knees deeply bent.
4 as the L toe picks the ice, extend body legs, then spring upward, swinging arms around in a curve to assist the turn.
5 make a complete turn in the air, holding arms close to body and crossing R foot over L foot.
6 land as in the Salchow, on LBO. The Lutz may also be done on the RBO.

split jump

The Lutz can also be turned into a split jump. The split – which can be either a sideways or a scissor-type split – is done at the peak of the elevation, just after the turn.

loop jump

1 begin preparation by skating on RFI, free foot to rear.
2 make an open Mohawk; turn. and shift to LBI, without making a bracket as in a normal Mohawk; keep free foot to rear.
3 reach into circle with R foot and skate toward the line being traced by the L foot until the two feet are aligned, R behind L.

4 take off by simultaneously lifting the L leg, raising the arms and stretching the R leg, then thrusting upward.
5 make a complete rotation, bringing the arms together in front of the body; cross the R foot over the L foot.
6 land as in a Salchow, on RBO.
The loop may also be done on the LBO.

Spins

There are three basic types of spin: upright, crouching, and horizontal. All spins must be done on the spot — that is, around a fixed point — and should include at least six rotations. You will probably find it easier to learn to spin in a counterclockwise direction. The instructions given here are for counterclockwise spin. An important thing to remember is that in going into a spin you should make a very tiny circle. Only when the spin is well-centered can you increase your speed; otherwise, the spin will travel in a corkscrew tracing over the ice. In coming out of a spin, fix your eyes on some stationary object. This will help to reduce dizziness.

Begin with the relatively simple two-footed upright spin, then move on to the others.

one-footed upright spin
1 begin the approach to the spin by skating on RBI.
2 change to LFO, making roughly a 90° angle to the previous tracing, and begin to skate a circle, keeping R foot well back.
3 about one-third of the way around the circle, cut into the circle, drawing the L arm back, and fix your eye on the point, just past the LA, where you will place the spin.
4a at LA you should be nearly at a stop. Bring R foot forward in an arc, and at the same time make a small three turn on the L foot.

two-footed upright spin
1 skate into the turn by first going forward on the LI edge.
2 bend knees and skate a semi-circle on the RFI, holding your arms next to your body.

3 turn L foot to BI edge to make a small inside spread-eagle position with R foot.
4 draw L foot close to R foot and straighten knees, turning around in a small circle and skating on the center of the blades. Accelerate the spin by folding the arms in close to the body.

b keeping R foot out to side, turn counterclockwise on the front of the L skate, with arms outstretched.
c once the spin is correctly centered on one spot, increase speed by bringing free foot in front of the knee of tracing foot.

d then fold arms in toward body and press free foot downward.
e to run out of spin swing free foot out to the side.
5 then thrust off with L foot and skate backward on RI edge.

sit spin

Begin the preparation for the sit spin as for the upright spin, steps 1 through 4a.

camel spin

1 begin preparation by skating on RBI as for sit spin and upright spin.

2 on LFO begin to make a circle as in preparation for other spins, but keep R foot on ice behind.

3 lift R foot off the ice and keep it well back, then cut into the circle as in preparation for the other spins.

4a after making the three turn and going into the spin, simultaneously raise R leg, lower torso, and stretch both arms out behind. Make the turn on the front of the full blade.

b come out of the spin by straightening up with R leg out to side. Then bend R leg and lower it. Complete the turn as for the other spins.

b bring the R foot out to the side as you move into the spin. Hold arms out to the side.
c swing the R leg around in front of the L leg, at the same time moving down into the sitting position. The spin is made on the full blade, on the forward part of the skate. In beginning the spin keep the arms away from the body.

d as you go into the full sitting position stretch the R leg out to the front, keeping the toe pointed. Fold the arms in front of the body. To accelerate the spin bring the arms closer to the body and cross the free foot in front of the tracing foot.

e to come out of the spin, straighten up on the L leg with R leg out to side.
f bend R leg, then gradually lower it, crossing the free foot in front of the tracing foot.
g bring the R foot out to the side and onto the ice.
5 thrust off with the L foot and skate backward on RO edge.

Planning your own free skating program is a challenge you'll probably enjoy. Here's your chance to create something unique — to take the known free skating steps, jumps, and spins and combine them in new, exciting ways to some of your favorite music. Free skating is one of the few art forms in which the performer and the creator are the same person.

Deciding on the content of your program — that is, on the movements to include, as opposed to how you arrange them — can be difficult. Obviously, a skater who executes a number of double jumps and tricky spins will have the advantage over one who sticks to single jumps and simpler movements — *provided* that the tricky movements are executed accurately and stylishly. So you should include the most difficult movements that you can do well. A program that's a little ambitious is probably better than one that lacks excitement. A few faults are to be expected, even in the big international competitions, though of course they will be counted against you. But a program that is mainly beyond your skating capability will look strained, so that the audience and judges will tend to watch you with anxiety, even when you're skating well.

Once you've chosen your music — which usually should include three or four selections of varied rhythm and tempo — plan the placing of your jumps and spins so that they occur at appropriate moments in the music. Generally speaking, you should try to space out the more spectacular movements in your program, giving them a "setting" with spirals, crossovers, little dance steps, and so on. But you can really create excitement by occasionally combining several jumps, one after the other, or a jump followed immediately by a spin. This gives your program an element of surprise and originality.

Remember that style is counted in judging your performance. Everyone has his or her own style — athletic, lyrical, dramatic — but all good skaters have in common certain basic aspects of style: head held high, but not stiffly; hands relaxed; neat footwork, which includes pointing the toes. Also, you should look as though you're enjoying yourself. Smiling occasionally will help to convey this, but it should certainly not be a fixed, artificial-looking smile. And be sure to bring your program to a sparkling finish with an elegant flourish or bow to your audience.

Done well, pair skating is a joy to watch. The man and woman move in perfect harmony and precision, separating then re-joining as smoothly as if drawn together by a magnet. Daring lifts and leaps, performed at high speed, give pair skating a dramatic quality unmatched in other kinds of skating.

Of course, it's difficult. You've not only got to be an excellent skater yourself, but you must also be able to adapt your own style to that of your partner. Teamwork is absolutely essential.

choosing a partner
Size is important. The girl should be a little smaller than the boy – partly because this looks better and partly to facilitate lifts. But a boy should not choose a partner who is much smaller than he is, because this would make the pair look unbalanced.

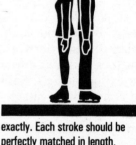

first steps together (below)
To begin with, you should practice skating together around the rink, both forward and backward, clockwise and counterclockwise. You'll find it easiest at first to skate side by side, the girl on the right, with the boy's right arm around her waist, her left arm around his waist, and his left hand holding hers. Work on coordinating all your movements exactly. Each stroke should be perfectly matched in length, depth of edge, and bend of knee. Movements of the head, shoulders, and arms should also be in unison.

practicing school figures

Although school figures are not included in pair skating competitions, it's important to practice these together. Tracing the circles, and learning how to do threes, brackets, and the other turns as a team will pay off in neat, synchronized footwork when you're free skating.

shadow skating

This is exactly what the name suggests: the two partners skating in unison, but without holding each other, so that one looks like the other's shadow. When you can shadow skate in perfect harmony you really are a team.

the waltz hold (below)

Once you can coordinate your movements while skating side by side, you should practice skating in the waltz position – facing each other, with the girl's left hand on the boy's right shoulder, his right hand a few inches above her waist, and her right hand in his. Coordinating your footwork is more difficult in this position, as you will normally be skating on opposite feet, and one partner will be skating forward while the other skates backward.

spirals (above)
Graceful and effective when done by an individual skater, spirals are even more beautiful done by a couple. They can be done either side by side or face to face, in a variety of postures, sometimes including a change of edge. Practice doing long spirals together. You may develop one that is uniquely yours that you can make a feature of your program.

separating (below)
Every pair skating team separates occasionally during a program. This injects variety into the program and also demonstrates their expert coordination, for it's very tricky to pace yourselves so that you get back together at the right place at the right moment so that your next steps dovetail exactly. In planning these separations make sure that your movements complement each other. You're still supposed to move as a team – not as a star and a supporting act. Also, avoid skating too far away from each other. This makes it difficult for the judges to watch both of you at the same time.

death spiral (above)
This is one of the most dramatic of all pair skating movements. To do it, the man pivots around on his left toe and RBO edge while holding the woman by the right hand. She is gradually lowered into a horizontal position, her head nearly touching the ice, while she skates a large circle around her partner. It's important for the man to keep his back straight and his free arm extended to create the balance required in this difficult maneuver.

three jump lift (below)
First a word of caution about lifts: They are difficult and dangerous and must be practiced under the guidance of a teacher. You can, however, practice them by yourselves off the ice, which will make them considerably easier on skates.
The three jump lift is one of the easier lifts and is seen frequently in pair skating programs.
1 skating in waltz position the man makes a three turn from RFI to RBO, while the woman turns from LBI to LFO.
2 the woman springs upward in a counterclockwise turn, while the man makes a half turn on the ice. As the woman begins her jump, she keeps her right hand low so that the man can push her upward with his left arm, adding height to the jump.
3 as the woman comes down on LBI, the man changes to LFO, continuing along the same curve as before the jump.

It was a natural development for ice skating to borrow some of the rhythms and steps of ballroom dancing, and so — quite a few years ago — ice dancing was born. Today it forms a part of national and international figure skating competitions.

Although ice dances use the same music as do the traditional ballroom dances — the waltz, foxtrot, tango, and others — they are very different in form. In ice dancing the couple move in a serpentine pattern around the rink, rather than going forward and backward and around in small circles as in most modern ballroom dances. For example, the basic step of the ballroom rumba is the box step, whereas the rumba danced on ice consists of a sequence of curves, making a sort of wavy oval tracing on the rink. Each dance has such a set pattern, which competitors must learn.

Ice dance competitors also perform a free dance — one in which they combine elements of the established dances, various free skating movements, and steps of their own devising in an imaginative program. This free dancing slightly resembles pair skating, but instead of the athletic feats characteristic of pair skating it features neat and often intricate footwork. Style is important in any kind of figure skating, but in ice dancing it is essential.

four dance holds

There are a number of different ways of holding your partner, which are used in varying combinations in the compulsory dances and in free dancing. The closed or waltz position (a) already described under pair skating (page 63) is one of the most frequently used.

A variation of the waltz hold is the tango hold (b), in which the skaters face opposite directions but position themselves hip to hip so that each one looks over the other's outstretched arm.

The foxtrot or open hold (c) uses basically the same arm positions as the waltz hold, but the partners face the same direction. It's important in this position that the man and woman keep their left and right shoulders, respectively, as far forward as possible, so that the space formed by their shoulders and outstretched arms is as narrow as possible.

In the kilian hold (d) the man and woman skate side by side in the same direction, usually with the woman on the right. The man places his right arm around the woman's waist and his hand on her right hip, and she places her right hand on top of his. Their left hands are clasped and held out to the side.

basic gliding step

This step is an essential part of ice dancing. In starting to learn it, take the kilian position so that you and your partner are skating in the same direction and using the same feet. Practice first on the full blade, then do the steps on a slight edge.

1 push forward on the left foot. Keep skating knee deeply bent and free foot stretched out behind, toe pointed.

2 gradually straighten the skating knee and bring the free foot up beside the skating foot.

3 bend both knees, keeping free foot just off the ice.

4 thrust off on right foot, and repeat movements (1) through (3). Each gliding step is thus made up of a down-up-down movement. In doing the step backward, carry the free foot in (1) stretched out in front of the skating foot.

running steps
Running steps resemble crossovers in that one foot continues the curve made by the other foot, and the outer foot may appear to be crossing over the inner foot – although in fact it does not.
1 thrust off with R inside edge onto LFO. Keep the skating knee bent throughout all the steps.

2 begin moving R foot forward past L foot.
3 bring R foot onto ice ahead of L foot and at the same time push backward and to the right side with L outside edge.
4 continue on RFI, with L foot behind and outside the tracing foot for a moment.
5 then bring L foot forward, passing R foot.
6 push off onto LFO and repeat steps 1 through 5.

When you've mastered this counterclockwise curve, practice running steps in a clockwise direction – RFO-LFI-RFO, and so on. Backward running steps are basically the reverse of forward runs, except that when the inner foot is raised, as in steps 3-4, it remains inside the line of the curve.

Ice dancing includes many of the free skating steps described earlier, such as the Mohawk, the Choctaw, and the spiral. A spiral done by two people, one skating forward, the other backward (a) is a very graceful movement.

chassés

The chassé used in ice dancing differs from the one used in free skating in that when the free foot is placed on the ice, the skating foot is lifted off the ice for a moment.
1 skate forward on LFO, with skating knee slightly bent.
2 bring R foot up to skating foot, parallel to it.

3 place R foot on the ice, on inside edge, and at the same time raise L foot off the ice, about as high as the depth of the blade, with R knee almost straight.
4 replace L foot on the ice and continue LFO curve.

cross chassé

In this variation of the chassé, the free foot is placed on the ice behind the skating foot and crossed over the line of the tracing. When skating backward, the free foot is crossed in front of the skating foot during the chassé.

In free dancing, you'll sometimes see the woman do a sliding step under her partner's arm (b) — a deft little movement that adds charm to a program.

Another frequently used step is a series of little kicking hops (c). These provide an interesting change of pace when inserted among smooth gliding steps.

Once you become fairly proficient at the ice dancing steps you can start learning some of the compulsory dances required in competitions. One of these is the foxtrot. The diagram shown opposite gives the step sequence for this dance. To a novice it looks rather complicated, but when you know the individual steps it makes much more sense.

There is also a simple dance done to the foxtrot beat, which is called the preliminary foxtrot, because it is required in preliminary tests of ice dancing proficiency. Learning this dance will help you master some of the basic principles of ice dancing. As you study the diagrams, keep in mind the beat of the music, which has four beats to the measure, with the main accent on the first beat. A tune such as "Mrs. Robinson" will give you the idea.

the foxtrot

The diagram reproduced here (by permission of the International Skating Union) shows the preferred pattern of steps for the foxtrot. The sequence of steps begins at one corner of the rink and is repeated at the corner diagonally opposite. The couple begin in the open position. At step 4 they assume the closed position, and at step 12 they again take the open position. The small wavy line indicates a short change of edge. The abbreviation x-roll means "cross roll," which is a change of edge and feet, producing a rolling motion, in which the free foot crosses over the skating foot during the change. All the other steps have already been described.

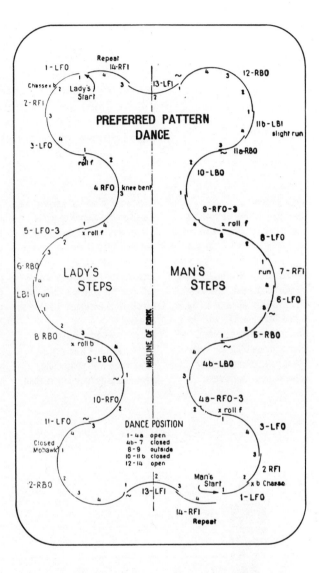

preliminary foxtrot

1 (first beat, first measure) start off with the girl on the right, holding hands, with your free hands out to the side. Push off with R foot and skate forward on LO edge. At the same time the man pulls his partner toward him so that by the next step they have assumed the kilian hold.

2 (second beat, first measure) make a running step onto the RI edge.

3 (third beat of measure) make another running step on LO edge. Hold this edge for the next three beats — that is, throughout beats 3 and 4 of the first measure, 1 and 2 of the second.

4 (third beat, second measure) skate forward on RO edge.

5 (fourth beat, second measure) make a running step onto LFI

6 (first beat, third measure) make a running step onto RO edge and hold for the remaining three beats of the measure. These 12 beats with accompanying steps make up the pattern of the dance, which is repeated around the rink.

Figure skating competitions, like other athletic events, are governed by established and detailed rules. There are three categories: single skating, pair skating, and ice dancing. All the events are skated on a rink measuring at least 63.4 by 28.4yd (58 by 26m) and no more than 65.6 by 32.8 yd (60 by 30m). There may be as many as nine judges, plus a referee and other officials.

single skating

The single skating competition consists of: compulsory figures, a short program, and a free skating program. The compulsory figures are chosen by the officials. They are skated in order of increasing difficulty. Each figure must be skated three times on each foot, with no pauses in between. Among the qualities the judges (a) look for are: correct posture, such as holding the hands palm downward (b) and (c) keeping the knee flexed; smooth, graceful movements; reasonable speed; and tracings that are the correct size, symmetrical, and accurately superimposed (d). Marks are deducted for skating on the flat of the blade (e) except at the start of a circle.

The short program consists of seven prescribed free skating movements with connecting steps and lasts for no more than two minutes. The skater chooses his own music and may perform the required movements in any order, but he may not add unprescribed movements to the program. The free skating program includes the skater's own choice of officially approved movements arranged as he pleases and skated to his own choice of music. The men's free skating program is five minutes long, the women's four minutes.

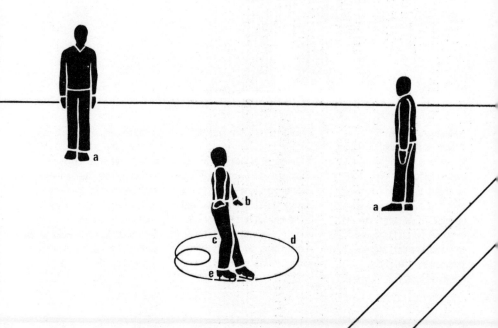

ice dancing
The competition consists of: compulsory dances, an original set pattern dance, and free dancing. The three compulsory dances may be chosen by the officials either the night before the competition or when the competition is announced. The rhythm of the set pattern dance is chosen by the Ice Dancing Committee of the International Skating Union, but the couple select their own music. The dance is composed of repetitive sequences consisting of either one half or one complete circuit of the rink. The couple may choose their own steps, provided that the movements conform to all the ISU rules. The free dance consists of non-repetitive combinations of dance movements arranged in a four-minute program set to the competitors' choice of music. The pair may use any dance movements and some free skating movements as well.

pair skating
The competition includes a short program including six compulsory movements and a five-minute free skating program. The man and woman need not perform the same movements or always remain in contact with each other, but they must give a united, harmonious performance. There are certain restrictions on movements in pair skating. For example, the man may lift his partner only by her torso (f), not by her arms or legs; he may not carry her for more than three revolutions; and he may not turn her in a horizontal position. In lifting her, his arm must be fully extended (g).

Most of the skating you're likely to see on television and in live performance is free skating or ice dancing. To the unsophisticated eye it all looks slightly miraculous, but as you watch more and more skating you'll begin to discriminate, which will increase your enjoyment. You'll begin to look at skating the way the judges do.

Two sets of marks are awarded for a program of free skating or ice dancing. One set is for technical merit, and the other is for artistic impression. The highest possible mark in either category is 6.0, which is rarely awarded. A row of 5.8s and 5.9s from the judges is remarkable and may mean the Gold Medal — provided the skater has also scored high on the compulsory figures.

technical merit
This phrase means exactly what it says. The skater is evaluated on the difficulty of the program and the skill with which it is performed. However, if a skater falls during a jump or other movement, that particular movement will not be marked. Among the things the judges consider are:

a minimum of two-footed skating; correct execution of the movements listed in the program submitted beforehand to the judges;
height in a jump (although some jumps, such as a three jump, are not meant to be high);
a smooth landing from a jump;
a spin that is well centered on the spot — one that doesn't "travel."

artistic impression
Ultimately, this is a matter of personal taste, but the judges' marks will usually show a fair amount of uniformity in evaluating this aspect of a program. The main thing to watch for is the way the skater matches the steps to the music – not only skating in time to it, but also interpreting it. A spectacular jump, for example, should coincide with a climax in the music. A drawn-out, graceful musical line should have its visual complement – perhaps a spiral or a slow spin.

A program is usually skated to several contrasting pieces of music, providing a variety of tempo and mood. One piece of music should seem to grow out of another naturally, and in shifting to the new tempo the skater should "change gear" smoothly.

Once you know the standard free skating movements, you'll enjoy noticing when a skater varies them or combines them in interesting ways. Some skaters display wit on the ice; some have a style reminiscent of classical ballet; some are flamboyant and acrobatic. Discovering your own favorites and following their progress from one competition to the next is one of the pleasures of watching skating.

For an advanced skater the goal is almost certainly to skate in the amateur championships — national and then perhaps international also. But whether or not you ever achieve such heights you may have the opportunity to go on enjoying your skating and also earn some money at it.

teaching

As ice skating grows in popularity there is more and more demand for teachers. Even quite young skaters can qualify as teachers, and for older skaters whose competing days are over, teaching provides its own compensations. Skating coaches share in the pride and excitement of their pupils' success and have the satisfaction of carrying on traditions while also introducing new ideas and techniques.

A new teaching aid — the hoist — helps young skaters learn to jump safely and with style.

ice shows

If you've ever watched one of the big ice shows you know that they provide work – and fun – for a lot of skaters. Besides the starring roles, these shows include plenty of group numbers. Of course ensemble work demands the very reverse of individualism; teamwork is the vital ingredient in this kind of skating. Performing in shows often involves being able to skate in elaborate costumes and handle props. The solo roles require the ability to express character while skating – in short, to act. Lines, if there are any, are usually spoken by actors and recorded in advance. But the skater must mouth the words at the same time and match the actions to them.

The lucky skater who combines superb skating technique with acting ability can have a dazzling – though usually rather short – career on the ice. You can discover whether or not ice show business is for you by taking part in one of the amateur shows put on by a local rink.

Figure skating on rollers

When the Olympia Roller Rink opened in London in 1910 it was the largest in the world.

The first roller skate is said to have been invented by a Belgian with the intriguing name of Merlin, back in 1760. For a long time roller skates were just a substitute for ice skates, used by skaters who wanted to practice during the warmer months of the year. Then in the late 1800s a ball-bearing skate with metal castors was developed and roller skating became a pastime in its own right. Today you can do just about anything on rollers that you can do on blades. Artistic roller skating demands just as much grace and precision as artistic ice skating. Recently, the roller disco has appeared on the scene, combining the fun of skating and dancing to the latest pop music.

skates
Strap-on skates are available at most rinks. You put them on over ordinary walking shoes — no fancy footwear.

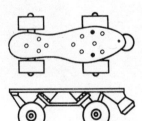

Once you've decided you really like skating you should buy good skates, and have them fitted to boots. The wheels of modern figure skates are made of wood, plastic, or nylon. The knob at the front of the skate is a toe stop. It serves much the same purpose as the toe pick on an ice skate, helping you to stop while skating backward and to perform certain jumps.

The roller skating boot is essentially the same as an ice skating boot. It should fit snugly, without being too tight in the toe.

clothing
Boys should wear pants and a shirt or sweater. When first learning to skate, girls, too, are well-advised to wear pants, as they protect the skin during falls. When you become a little more expert you can wear a skating skirt or dress and tights. Beginning skaters should not wear a wristwatch on the rink, as it might be damaged during a fall.

rinks

Roller skating rinks have various kinds of skating surface: asphalt, cement, wood, and wood covered with polyurethane, which makes for quiet skating. As on an ice rink, skaters move in a counter-clockwise direction. Circles painted on the floor provide the tracings used in skating compulsory figures.

First steps and edges

Many people learn to roller skate, after a fashion, as children, and can go straight on to learning about edges, figures and free skating movements. But if you've never been on rollers before, you'll first have to learn to keep your balance, to glide forward easily, and to come to a graceful stop.

walking
First practice simply walking forward.
1 start with the feet about 6in (15cm) apart and the knees bent slightly.
2 then lift one foot and put it down a very short way ahead of the other. Repeat. Turn your toes out slightly and move in time to the music.

gliding (above)
Next, practice moving forward on one foot.
1 push off gently on the right foot and hold the left foot slightly behind and above the right. Count to three as you glide forward.
2 bring the left foot down beside the right and push forward on it. Glide forward to a count of three. Repeat.

1 now try gliding forward as before, but instead of bringing the free foot down beside the tracing foot,
2 bring it down with the heel in front of the instep of the tracing foot, making a "T."
3 propel yourself forward by pushing with the rear foot, using the inside front and back wheels of the skate – not just the toe.

Extend the pushing leg straight behind you and only slightly off the rink.

stopping (below)
The easiest way to stop while skating forward is the T-stop. (Backward skating and stopping are explained on pages 86-87.)
1 while gliding forward on one foot, bring the free foot up behind it in the "T" position.
2 lower the free foot gently and gradually shift some of your weight onto it, braking yourself to a stop.

edges (below)
In order to skate in curves you must skate on the inner or outer wheels of the skate. You do this by leaning to one side or the other, so shifting your weight to that side. The wheels on which your weight is resting will then turn slightly toward each other, which causes the skate to move in a curved line. As in artistic ice skating, the various edges are referred to as RFO (right forward outside), LBI (left back inside), and so on.

First practice moving forward on right and left inside edges. These are easier to learn than outside edges, because your free foot is in a position to help you regain your balance should you start to wobble. Once you can do a forward inside edge with some confidence, work on your outside forward edges.

Once you've learned how to skate forward and have mastered the forward edges, you should learn to skate on a backward edge. Then you should learn to do crossovers. These are useful in getting you around the corners of the rink, and they're also very graceful movements, used often in free skating programs.

skating backward (below)
1 start by standing with your toes together and your heels turned slightly outward. Keep your knees bent.
2 push forward on the inside edge of the left foot and glide backward on the outside edge of the right foot, at the same time straightening the left knee, so that the free foot is forward, toe pointed. Hold for a count of 3.

3 bring the free foot back beside the tracing foot.
4 straighten your right knee and lower the left foot onto the floor, shifting your weight to that foot.
5 push forward with the inside edge of the right foot and glide backward on the outside edge of the left. Repeat.

backward stops (below)
To stop when skating backward, move your free leg behind the tracing leg and place the toe stop on the rink. Keep your weight forward and let the toe stop brake you gradually to a standstill.

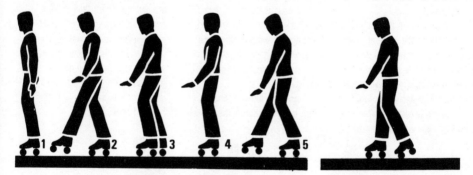

forward crossovers (below)
1 start by skating on LFO.
2 now, keeping the knees well bent, bring your right foot forward, ahead of the tracing foot. At the same time bring forward your right arm, shoulder, and hip, and bring back your left arm, shoulder, and hip.

3 bring the right skate in front of and across the left skate and gradually shift your weight to RFI.
As weight shift is completed, slide left foot out behind, outside the curve.
4 bring left foot back up beside right foot.

5 shift weight to LFO, pushing off with right, and continue forward. Repeat.
For clockwise crossovers, reverse these directions.

backward crossovers (below)
1 start by skating on RBO, keeping the left leg extended forward and the right knee bent.
2 now bring the left leg back and cross it in front of the right leg, while keeping the left arm, shoulder, and hip forward and the right shoulder and arm back.

3 shift your weight to LBI and swing the right foot out behind you, slightly outside the curve, with toe pointed.
4 bring right foot up beside left foot.
5 shift weight to RBO, push off with left foot, and continue backward. Repeat. For clockwise backward crossovers, reverse these directions.

The figures done in ice figure skating can also be done on roller skates. They are performed on circles painted onto the rink surface and must be started from a stationary position. Learning to do a curve eight will give you a good idea of the basic principles involved.

curve eight – RFO–LFO
1 stand at the intersection of the two circles with right foot pointing along the line of the circle to your right, and left foot at right angles to it, making a "T." Your right shoulder, arm, and hip should be forward, your left shoulder, arm, and hip back.
2 push off with inside edge of left foot onto RFO, keeping your tracing knee bent and extending the free leg behind you. Look over your right shoulder in the direction of travel.

3 at about a third of the way around the circle, begin moving the free leg forward, but keep the free shoulder, arm, and hip turned back.
4 at about two-thirds of the way around the circle, the free foot should be extended in front of the tracing foot. Begin bringing the free arm, shoulder, and hip forward also, and gradually bring the free foot back to a position just ahead of tracing foot.
At the intersection of the two circles you will have completed

the rotation of the body and will be ready to change to the left foot.
5 place the left foot on the rink and at the same time push back strongly with the right inside edge.
6 complete the second circle on LFO, reversing the movements described for the first circle.

A figure skater traces a loop over one painted on the floor.

For many people free skating is the most enjoyable kind of skating. It includes all sorts of interesting, graceful, and very spectacular movements and gives the skater an opportunity to interpret music in his or her own distinctive way.

Here are a few of the many free skating steps you can learn.

three turn (above)
This is one of several steps used to change direction. When executed at the half-way mark on a circle it makes the compulsory figure known simply as a "three" (see pages 34-35). The turn itself is often used in free skating and dancing programs.
To skate a forward three turn:

1 skate on RFO, with left foot and right shoulder and arm back and left arm crossed in front of body.
2 exaggerate the arm positions and lean strongly into the curve with tracing knee well bent.
3 make the turn by simultaneously straightening the knees, bringing the free foot close

to the heel of the tracing foot, rotating the shoulders, and rolling off the front of the skate in a slight rocking motion onto the RBI. Bend the tracing knee.
4 continue the curve on RBI. The three turn can also be made from LFO to LBI, and from a backward to a forward edge.

Mohawk (right)
This is a two-footed turn that traces a path similar to that of a three turn. There are several kinds of Mohawk, distinguished by whether or not the feet cross each other, and whether the free foot is kept forward after the turn or swung back. These

instructions are for an open, crossed Mohawk, from LFO to RBO.
1 skate on LFO with free leg extended behind and tracing knee bent. Tracing shoulder and arm are forward, free shoulder and arm back.

2 to make the turn, bring the free foot up beside the tracing foot with the heel against the tracing foot instep, forming a "T."
3 shift weight onto right foot and skate backward on RO edge, with tracing knee bent and free leg swung out behind.

Keeping your balance is as tricky on rollers as on blades.

the teapot (above)
This novel free skating movement is a good one for acquiring balance and flexibility.
1 skate forward on both feet with knees bent and arms extended straight out in front of body.
2 continuing to skate forward, crouch down, keeping your body forward over your skates.

3 as you reach the squatting position, extend one leg forward with the skate off the rink surface, and grasp the leg near the ankle with both hands. The teapot can also be done while skating backward.

three jump (above)
Before you try this jump, just practice jumping on both feet. Skate forward with the feet parallel and close together. Bend the knees deeply, swing your arms out in front of you, and jump. Bend your knees as you land. Once you can land easily with your weight evenly over both feet, try the three jump.

two-foot spin (above)
This spin is a good one to begin with, as it's not too difficult. In time you will get over being dizzy while spinning.
1 skate forward on both feet.
2 shift all your weight to one foot and slowly lift the other foot to one side.
3 now lower the free foot until the front wheels of the skate just touch the rink surface. This will cause you to spin.

1 skate forward on LO edge, with tracing knee well bent, free foot, shoulder, and arm back, and tracing shoulder and arm forward.
2 bring both arms forward and upward, and at the same time thrust upward strongly with the tracing leg, bring free leg forward, and make one-half revolution in the air.
3 land on RBO with right knee deeply bent, right arm to rear, left arm forward, and left leg back to side.

As in ice figure skating, there are three categories in which a roller skater may choose to compete: individual skating, pair skating, and dance skating.

individual skating

If you compete as an individual skater you will be required to execute several of the compulsory figures, which include eights, loops, threes, rockers, counters, and brackets.

Each figure must be repeated three times consecutively. Turns must be skated with a clean edge, without skids, scrapes, noise, or lifting of the wheels. Posture is an important factor in judging the figures. The skater's head should be held upright and the arms held gracefully with the palms relaxed and parallel to the floor. Both knees must be slightly bent, and the free foot should be held just off the rink surface, not too near the tracing foot, with the toe pointed downward and outward.

In the free skating part of the competition skaters perform their own selection of movements to music of their choice. The length of the program varies with the competition.

If a skater falls through no fault of his own (for example, on an object left on the rink), he is allowed to restart. A skater who falls through his own fault will have his marks adjusted accordingly and must continue from where he fell.

Three sets of marks are awarded: one for the compulsory figures, one for the content and difficulty of the free skating program, and one for the manner in which it is performed.

In each case the marks range from 1 to 6, with intermediate decimal places. The three sets of marks are totaled to determine the winner and runners-up.

dance skating
There are two parts to the dance skating competition: the performance of two, three, or four compulsory dances, depending on the competition, and a program of free dancing. Some of the requirements for the compulsory dances are that the couple should skate close together and execute all the movements in unison, make all steps accurately, and coordinate all movements with the music.

In the free dancing the couple may combine a variety of movements including variations of known dances or parts of dances and various free skating movements. Unnecessary feats of strength or skating skill are counted against the dancers. They may separate only long enough to change positions. Spins may not exceed 1½ revolutions. Jumps and lifts in which the man's hands are higher than the waist are not permitted.

Competitors receive marks (ranging from 0 through 6) for each of the compulsory dances, for the content and difficulty of their free dancing program and for its manner of performance.

pair skating
Competitors in this category perform a free skating program and receive two sets of marks, as for individual free skating. They must give an impression of unison, though they need not perform the same movements and may separate occasionally. They are always judged as a pair, not as individuals.

Speed skating

Road racing is a popular form of moving fast on roller skates.

As early as the 13th century the Dutch were racing on blades over frozen canals, but the first recorded speed skating competition was in 1676. Probably by this time speed skating had spread to other countries. Dutch people who settled in England's Fen country in the 16th century may have introduced the sport in that area, where it remains popular to this day.

The early races were run on straight tracks, but around the late 1800s U-shaped and then oval tracks began to be used. Speed skating is an open-air sport because the length of the track — usually 437yd(400m) — makes it too large to be conveniently accommodated indoors. (Indoor rinks are, however, used for short track speed skating.) Artificial refrigeration makes it possible to hold races when the weather is mild, but because of its cost it is used only on the major championship tracks. Most speed skaters, therefore, depend on natural ice, so it is hardly surprising that most of the champions come from countries with cold climates. High altitudes also help, for the thinner air improves the skater's performance. Most of the world records have been set at rinks located 547yd(500m) or more above sea level.

Speed skaters may average 30mph(48kph), making them the fastest self-propelled humans on a level surface. Skaters on rollers are nearly as fast as those on blades.

The first officially recognized world speed ice skating championships were held in Amsterdam in 1893, and the first roller skating world championships in Monza, Italy, in 1937. The previous year, the first women's ice racing championships were held in Stockholm. Today some of the top speed skaters, on both blades and rollers, are women.

A speed skater leans forward to cut down wind resistance.

Speed skating on ice

Ice skating races cover varying distances, from 547yd(500m) to 6.2ml(10,000m) or more. Women's races may be up to 1.86ml(3000m) in length. Two skaters at a time race in a counter-clockwise direction around the track. Points are given in relation to the skater's time in each event. The overall winner is the skater who wins three of the four distances raced or who has the lowest total of points.

the rink
An international speed skating track measures up to 437yd(400m) in length and has two lanes, each 4.4 or 5.5yd(4 or 5m) wide. The lanes are divided by snow or by a painted line on which rubber blocks are placed at intervals. Skaters must change lanes along the crossing straight section of the track.

officials
These include a referee and assistant referee, a starter and assistant starter, a chief timekeeper and four timekeepers, lap scorers, track stewards and a crossing controller.

a start 500m
b finish 1000m
c start 10,000m, finish 500m, 1500m, 3000m, 5000m, 10,000m
d start 1500m
e start 1000m
f start 3000m, 5000m

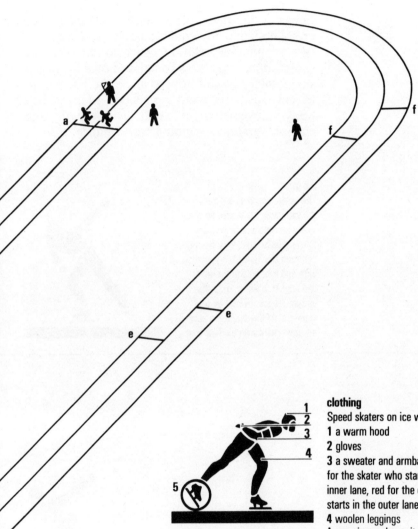

clothing
Speed skaters on ice wear:
1 a warm hood
2 gloves
3 a sweater and armband (white
for the skater who starts in the
inner lane, red for the one who
starts in the outer lane)
4 woolen leggings
A one-piece nylon suit with a
hood attached is a common
modern alternative.

skates
Racing skates (5) have long thin
straight blades measuring from
12 to 18 inches (30 to 45cm),
reinforced with steel tubing along
the upper edge. The shoe is made
of thin leather for lightness, with
the heel slightly raised and
directly over the blade.

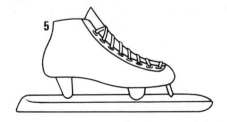

Speed skating techniques

Speed skating is much simpler than figure skating — which is not to say that it's *easier!* Fewer techniques are involved, because there's really only one objective: to cover the distance as fast as possible. But in order to do this, the skater must know how to balance over his or her skate correctly and how to angle the body so as to cut down its wind resistance. Many subtle body movements, as well as strength and stamina, go into a winning performance.

the start

The skater assumes a position at the start with his blades as close to the starting line as possible. Starting techniques vary from the common semi-crouching position with one foot behind the other and angled to the side, to the upright stance favored by top sprinters. At the signal, he pushes off powerfully with his rear foot.

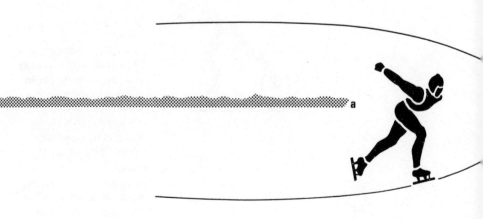

a

gaining speed
On each glide forward the skate strikes the ice at an angle of about ten degrees, making a rolling motion from the outside edge to the inside edge during the glide.

The skater's body is well balanced over the skating leg, with the free leg held out behind. The clasping of the hands behind the back is not just a trick to make the skating look effortless; it's a way of conserving energy and at the same time streamlining the body to lower its wind resistance.

turning corners
In skating around the curves at each end of the track the skater does crossovers. These are essentially the same as those described on page 24, though of course the body position is different, and the longer length of the skate makes the placement of the feet slightly more difficult to master.

changing lanes
In order to give each skater an equal chance, the rules require them to change lanes each time they reach the crossing straight section of the track. The only exception to this is when skating the first straight of the 1000m or 1500m race on a 400m track. The lanes are marked either with a painted line on which rubber blocks are placed at intervals or with a narrow strip of loosely packed snow (a) which can be crossed easily.

As the name implies, this kind of racing is held on a relatively small track — compared to the outdoor variety — and the races cover relatively short distances. The individual races may cover distances of 437-3280yd(400-3000m) and are run according to a heat system or an elimination system. Other short track events are relay races with teams of four skaters and pursuit races between two skaters.

individual races (1)
In the heat system (a) a maximum of four skaters race together in short distance events; a maximum of eight in long distance events. Skaters may qualify for further rounds by either: winning a heat; being among a specified number of skaters with the fastest times; or being among the fastest runners-up. The race winner is the first skater to finish in the final.
In the elimination system (b) a maximum of eight skaters compete. Another skater is eliminated after the next two laps and after each successive two laps until only the winner remains.
The leading competitor has the right of way and may only be passed on the outside, provided he keeps to the inside of the track. The responsibility for any collision or obstruction is with the skater who is overtaking.

1a

1b

relay races (2)
Teams have four members, each of whom must take part. Only one competitor at a time from each team may skate in a race until relieved.
A skater may be replaced by another member of the team at any time except during the last two laps. The incoming team member is not in the race until he has touched, or is touched by, the skater who is being replaced. The team of the first skater to reach the finishing line wins the race.

pursuit races (3)
Each race is between two skaters. They start opposite each other, each in the middle of the straight. Each race lasts a minimum of 10 laps. The winner is the skater who overtakes the other one or who finishes in the faster time. Heat winners qualify for the next round, in which the fastest qualifier is matched against the slowest qualifier, and the second fastest against the second slowest, and so on, until the winner is determined.

Basically similar to speed skating on ice, roller racing is held on both outdoor and indoor tracks, covering long and short distances, and sometimes on open roads. In America specially constructed 'banked' tracks are used for Roller Derbies.

Individual races

The width of the track limits the number of skaters that can take part in a heat. Widths range from 8ft(2.4m) for two skaters to 20ft(6m) for six skaters. Races are run counterclockwise around the track. The leading skater has the right of way and may only be overtaken on the outside as long as he keeps to the inside of the track.

A skater who has been, or is being, lapped may be ordered to give way. The judges will signal to him with a yellow flag, and the skater must then go to the outside of the track without impeding any other competitor. If he has been lapped twice by the leading skater he may be signalled to leave the track. The winner is the first skater to reach the finishing line.

Relay races

These can take place on the same track as is used for individual races. In relay races two skaters – one from each team – skate around the track until they are relieved by another skater from their respective teams. Every member of the team must take part. Takeovers are by touch and are permitted at any point in the race except during the last two laps.

Roller derby

The roller derby track measures 100 to 200ft(91.4 to 182.9m) in total length and is usually made of hardwood with a plastic coating to prevent slipping. Two teams, consisting of five men and five women, take turns racing around the track for 12 minutes at a time. Points are gained by lapping opponents. Skaters may change lanes at will, and although tripping is prohibited, pushing and jostling are both allowed, making roller derby a fairly rough sport.

Road races

Using carefully resurfaced public roads, or motor race tracks, roller speed skaters compete in events similar to ice speed skaters. The longer stretches of straight road, than those possible on indoor tracks enable the skater to reach faster speeds.

Games on skates

A moment in an ice hockey game between Czechs and Russians.

Ice hockey is certainly the fastest of all team sports, and for many people the most exciting. In professional games, the puck may travel at speeds of up to 100 miles per hour. The sport combines the exhilaration of speed skating with the competitive pleasure of scoring goals — often against very tough opposition.

The first game of ice hockey played according to established rules was held at McGill University in Montreal in 1875, but the game had been played in Canada for some years before that. British soldiers were playing it in Kingston, Ontario, in the 1850s. It may have derived from bandy, an ice game played in England for many years, but it also resembles various other games, such as curling, field hockey, and lacrosse.

Whatevery its origins, ice hockey soon spread from Canada — where it is still the national sport — to the United States and Europe. By the early 1970s there were 230,000 players in Canada and 300,000 in the USSR. In North America there are several professional hockey leagues, the major one being the National Hockey League, which includes both American and Canadian teams. The number of amateur hockey teams is steadily increasing. In the United States today more than a million boys, some as young as eight years old, are learning to play this exciting game.

There were plenty of spills in early ice hockey, as this 19th century American print shows.

Being one of the roughest of all team sports, ice hockey demands a considerable amount of protective clothing. You may feel awkward in it at first, but in time you'll get used to it. Failing to wear an item of protective clothing might result in an injury that would keep you off the ice for a long time, so don't take chances. Although professional hockey teams don't wear helmets, young players are well-advised to do so. A mouthpiece to protect your teeth is essential.

clothing
1 long underwear absorbs perspiration.
2 protective cup, shoulder and chest pads.
3 shin pads are covered by stockings, held up by a garter belt; elbow pads are very important.
4 pants are held up by suspenders.
5 shirt and skates.
6 helmet and gloves.

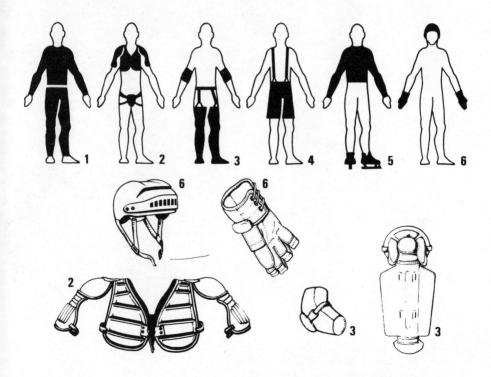

hockey stick

Hockey sticks come in a range of sizes, with the blade at various angles to the shaft of the stick. This angle is called the "lie." The smaller the angle, the higher the number of the lie. Most players are comfortable with a lie of 5 or 6, but if you tend to play in a very hunched-over position, you might want a 3 or 4. You can buy a stick with a blade angled to the right or to the left, if you prefer, instead of a vertical blade. Tape around the blade will help you to control the puck, and tape on the handle gives you a better grip.

goalkeeper's equipment

The goalie wears about 40lb (18kg) of equipment, including massive pads and a mask. On one hand he wears a catching glove (top right) and on the other a stick glove (top left). The goalkeeper's stick (b) is larger than the regular stick (a). (bottom) goalkeeper wearing pads, mask and gloves.

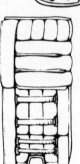

hockey skates

Only skates specifically designed for hockey may be worn. All players except goalies must wear skate heel guards. Buy skates that are comfortably snug for good support, and buy the best you can possibly afford – they're your most important article of equipment.

the rink

Ice hockey is played on a rink measuring approximately 67yd(61m) long by 28 or 33yd(26 or 30m) wide. A red line (a) divides the playing area in half, and two blue lines (b) on either side of it enclose each team's defending zone (the opposing team's attacking zone). At each end of the rink is a goal (c), behind which is a goal judge's box. The center circle (d) is the area where play is started, with a "face-off." Other face-off circles (e) may be used in resuming play after it has been stopped. The rink is surrounded by a wall approximately 4ft(1.2m) high (f) called the "boards."

the goal crease

The marked area in front of the goal is called the goal crease. It is curved for international matches, but on some rinks it is rectangular. An attacking player may not be in the goal crease when the puck passes over the goal line.

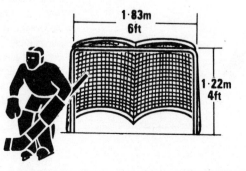

33yd
30m

1·83m
6ft

1·22m
4ft

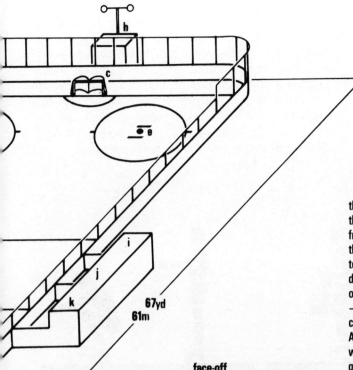

67yd
61m

the team

Each team may have as many as 15 players, of whom only six — three forwards, two defensemen and a goalkeeper — may be on the ice at one time. Remaining players sit on the bench (g) and may be substituted for players on the rink at any time.

duration of game

The game consists of three 20-minute periods of actual playing time, with 10 minutes' break between each period. Play is not stopped for substitutions.

face-off

Play begins with a face-off in the center circle. The referee drops the puck between the two opposing players onto the face-off spot marked on the rink. Each player stands facing his opponents' end, about one stick-length away from the face-off spot, and with his stick on the ice on his side of the spot. No other player may enter the circle during face-off. Players must not touch the puck until it reaches the ice.

scoring

A goal is scored when the puck crosses the line connecting the two goalposts. One point is awarded for each goal and one for an assist.

A goal and assist(s) are scored when: (1) an attacker legally puts the puck into the goal with his stick — in which case an assist is credited to the player or players (maximum two) who took part in

the play preceding the shot; or (2) the puck is deflected into the goal from the shot of an attacker off the stick, person, or skates of a teammate (provided it was not deliberately kicked, thrown, or otherwise directed into the goal) — in which case the assist is credited to the shooting player. A goal but no assist is scored when: (1) the puck is put into the goal in any way by a defender; or (2) an attacker kicks the puck and it is deflected into the net by a defender other than the goalkeeper.

A goal may also be awarded to a team if the opposing team violates the rules in certain ways. The team scoring the most points wins the game. Usually, if the score is even at the end of the third period a tie is declared.

officials

There must be: two neutral referees (international rules), or one referee and two linesmen (national rules); two goal judges (h); game timekeeper (i); penalty timekeeper (j); official scorer (k).

A game as strenuous as ice hockey demands a body in excellent condition. There are any number of exercises you can do to increase your strength and stamina and to improve your skating ability. Off the ice, you can develop your leg muscles and improve your breathing by running. Push-ups and sit-ups — which can be done on the rink — are also good exercises. Always limber up on the ice before a game.

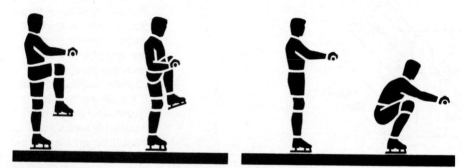

knee pull (above left)
This exercise is good for balance and also for the arms and shoulders. While skating forward slowly, with the stick held horizontally, raise one knee so that it is just behind the stick. Then use the stick to pull the knee toward the chest. Release and repeat. Then repeat with the other leg.

knee bend (above right)
While skating forward on both feet, with the feet about a skate-length apart, and holding the stick horizontally, crouch down and bounce several times. This exercise is particularly good for goalkeepers, who must often squat low on the ice to block a shot.

running over sticks
Lay the sticks parallel on the ice and run over the ice holding a stick, avoiding the sticks placed on the ice. This exercise will help you improve your balance.

running sideways (below)
Do this exercise with the rest of
your team. Line up at one end of
the rink. Then at the signal run
sideways – that is, diagonally –
toward the other end. Face
straight ahead as you run – not
in the direction you're moving.
This exercise is good for
developing maneuverability as
well as power.

stickhandling exercise
Place some chairs on the ice at
intervals of 10-12ft(3-3.6m).
Then stickhandle your way
around the chairs from one end of
the rink to the other. This will
train you not to look at the puck,
for if you do, you will collide with
a chair.

Any hockey expert will tell you that skating is the most important part of the game. To play really well you must be able to skate as easily as you walk. But you must also be adept at handling the puck and outwitting the opposition.

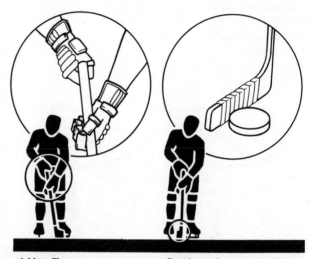

holding the stick
Hold the stick firmly in both hands, letting your fingers and thumbs – not your palms – do the work. Be sure to keep the stick close to the surface of the ice, so that you're ready to receive the puck if it's passed to you. In receiving, you should cup the blade over the puck to keep it under control.

stickhandling
If the way ahead is clear, you can push the puck over the ice keeping it cupped under the stick (in this case, you can hold the stick with one hand). But if the opposition is in the way, you must stickhandle the puck – that is, push it quickly from side to side, a few inches on each sweep. You must be able to do this with your head up, not looking down.

Practice until you can do this. Don't run with the puck carried out to one side; this will reduce your ability to pass or shoot in any direction.

skating skills

Many different skating skills are required in playing hockey. "Free skating" is simply the forward skating you use to cover a distance when no one's in the way. Work on developing a powerful push that will send you forward in long, fast glides. Keep your knees well bent and your body angled slightly forward. You must be able to skate backward well when you're checking a puck carrier or covering an opponent.

Agility is all-important to a hockey player. Practice doing crossovers (see Chapter 1) in both directions so that you can turn easily either way. "Cutting" is the technique of skating sharply to the side — useful in eluding an opponent. Practice the hockey stop described in Chapter 1, which will enable you to stop quickly.

faking

Besides being able to turn quickly on your skates, you must be able to fool an opponent into thinking you're about to move one way so that you can immediately move, or pass, or shoot the other way. The faking moves you use for this are called "dekes" and are of primary importance in offensive play.

It's important to be able to pass and receive the puck both forehand and backhand. And when you're passing, try to anticipate the place where your teammate's stick will be a split second later. If you pass to the point where it is at that instant he will have moved past the point by the time the puck gets there.

sweep pass
Move the puck with a firm but smooth sweeping action, keeping the stick on the ice, and follow through. (That is, continue the swing in the same path after striking the puck). This pass is used when you have a fair amount of time in which to set it up.

flip pass
This pass is used to get the puck over some obstacle, usually an opponent's stick. Use the toe of the blade and a quick upward rotation of the wrists.

slap pass
This pass is used when you receive the puck in the middle of a scramble and want to send it on quickly to another teammate. Bring the stick back a short way, then send it forward quickly, hitting the puck sharply.

snap pass
Use this pass to send the puck on its way in a hurry. A quick snap of the wrists does it. This is an important pass to master so that you can take the opposition by surprise.

drop pass
This is a way of sending the puck to a teammate who's behind you. Carry the puck forward, then quickly move the stickblade in front of the puck and give it a sharp slap. This stops its forward movement and leaves it on the ice for the other player.

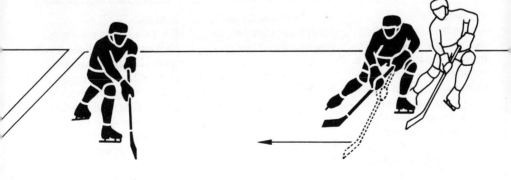

Shooting goals is, of course, the point of the game. There are several shots you can use, depending on the position you're in, the position of the goalkeeper, and other factors. Try to aim for one of the four corners of the goal — preferably the one with the largest amount of net showing.

slap shot
This is a very powerful, exciting shot, but not so accurate. Move the lower hand down the stick so that the two hands are about 20in (50cm) apart. Your head should be over the puck. Swing the stick back and upward, keeping your eye on the puck, then bring it down fast and hard. The blade should strike the ice about an inch or two behind the puck. As you hit the puck you shift your weight to the front foot.

wrist shot
This is a fast and effective shot, made with a powerful snap of the wrists. The hands should be 12-15in(30-37cm) apart on the stick and the puck to the side of the body. Drag the puck toward the goal, keeping it in the middle of the blade. Just before shooting, the wrists should be

backhand wrist shot

It's important to be able to shoot backhand, because you'll often find yourself in a position in which moving the puck to make a forehand shot may lose you the puck. Also, backhand shots are more apt to take the goalie by surprise. Essentially, the movements are the same as for the forehand wrist shot, though reversed, of course. But the upper hand follows the lower hand, rather than pulling back during the shot.

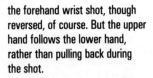

cocked back away from the goal. Then, while continuing to skate forward, push the lower hand forward and up in a quick snapping motion, and at the same time pull the upper hand back. Follow through, transferring the weight to the front foot.

flip shot

This shot is very useful when the goalie is lying in front of the goal, or when you're in a scramble around the net. Hold the stick with the hands about 12in(30cm) apart. The puck should be toward the toe of the blade and the blade should be either vertical or angled slightly away from the puck. Strike the puck with a snap of the wrists, using a lifting action.

It's generally agreed that the goalkeeper has the most important position on the team. He must be alert every second that the puck is in his team's defensive area and must have quick reflexes, for the puck may come at him at up to 100 mph (160kph). He must also be a good skater so that he can move across the goal quickly. A vital part of the job is narrowing the angle — placing yourself nearer the puck carrier so that you shield more of the net from his eyes.

stance
When you're waiting for the puck to come your way stand with your knees slightly bent and lean forward. You can keep your legs spread apart or stand with your shin pads touching. Hold the stick just above the wide section of the shaft, with the blade in front of your skates, and keep the catching mitt open and ready.

covering shots
An offensive player will usually aim for one of four corners of the goal. If the shot is to one of the upper corners, you raise your glove or stick to deflect it. If it's low, you must quickly crouch down on the ice and use your glove, stick, or leg pads.

moving across the goal

Obviously, you'll often have to move very quickly from one side of the goal to the other. Practice skating back and forth between the posts. If you're moving to the left, turn your left skate toward the post and push off hard with the right. If the puck is around to one side of the net, stand right next to the post on that side with the outside skate covering the corner. That way, you can block a shot coming from the side.

sliding

Sometimes you'll have to lie down across the goal to block a shot. But then you must be able to get up quickly to counter the next move. When you slide on the ice try to avoid having a leg in the air, and hold the stick along the ice to cover as much of the distance as possible.

All players must be able to check, but this skill is especially important for defensemen. There are two general types of checking: stick checking and body checking. You may body check only if the player has the puck or is the one who had it last. Otherwise the move is considered interference and is subject to a minor penalty.

Another important defense tactic is covering. This consists of skating close to an attacking player to prevent his gaining control of the puck.

sweep check (above)
This is a more difficult maneuver, in which you must crouch or kneel on the ice and lay the stick flat on it. Then you sweep the puck away from the attacker. This check is something of a gamble, for if it fails, the attacker can easily skate right by you and you've lost your chance to body check him.

poke check (below)
This is the most effective way of regaining the puck. To do it, you release one hand from the stick and with the other hand give a quick jab either at the puck carrier's stick or at the puck itself. Surprise is important. Wait until the puck carrier gets near you, then check.

pressing (left)
If the puck carrier is ahead of you, you can sometimes dislodge the puck by pressing your stick against his stick or against his gloves. This may cause him to lose control of the puck. But beware of slashing at him, which will get you a penalty.

stick lift (left)
To execute this check you should be behind or beside the puck carrier. You place your stick under his and lift it.

shoulder check (below)
To shoulder check, you skate up to your opponent – using no more than two strides – keeping your knees well bent and your weight on the inside edges of your skates.Then push your shoulder into the shoulder or chest of your opponent. Keep your eyes on your opponent, and be sure not to use your elbows.

hip check (below)
This is a slightly trickier move than the shoulder check. It is used to best advantage when the puck carrier is between you and the board, so that he can't easily change course. As he skates past you, move into him, keeping the closer leg bent and the outer leg out straight, and thrust your hip into his stomach area.

Because ice hockey is such a fast game, strategy is usually a matter of making split-second decisions. The situation changes at lightning speed, so that players must remain constantly alert and ready to change their strategy without even a moment's notice.

On the simplest level, all players must be prepared to switch quickly from attack to defense and back. Of course it is the forwards' main responsibility to score goals and the defensemen's and goalie's responsibility to prevent the other team from scoring. But the team as a whole is on the attack when it has the puck and on the defense when the other team has it. Since the puck rarely remains in one team's possession for more than about 30 seconds, it's obvious that flexibility is crucial.

There are virtually an infinite number of situations and possible plays in hockey. Here are just a few pointers for the beginning player.

face-offs

In the course of a game there may be 50 or more face-offs. Usually they are taken by the center. He plans the strategy and sets up his teammates accordingly. Getting control of the puck at the outset gives you the initiative and a better chance of scoring. Keep your eye on the linesman and try to move with him as he drops the puck.

If the face-off is at the center, you should try to pass it back to one of the defensemen, then skate forward, ready to receive a pass from the defenseman and carry the puck on up the ice. If you can manage to trick your opponent into thinking you'll pass one way, then pass quickly in the other direction, so much the better. If the face-off is in your attacking zone, your team should be prepared to win the draw and go for a goal quickly. In this situation, you might pass to a wing, or you might shoot at the goal yourself.

If the face-off is in your defending zone, your team should be prepared to lose the draw, so that each player is ready to check an opponent and prevent a goal if the other team does get control of the puck.

offensive play

Up to their attacking blue line the forwards should concentrate on getting the puck forward as fast as possible, passing to a man in the clear, rather than stickhandling. They should attack on a wide front; the wings generally should stay on their side of the ice. Once in the attacking zone, one of the forwards should at all times be in a good position to score. Passes should be made only to teammates who are uncovered.

A puck-carrying defenseman tries mainly to pass the puck up to an open teammate, stickhandling only when everyone else is covered. Once he makes a pass, he follows on up the ice, ready to receive a return pass or cover a possible interception.

defensive play

In a defensive situation, with the puck in the opponents' end, one of the forwards — usually the center — forechecks the puck carrier. Or two forwards may go after him while the third covers the nearest open opponent to prevent his receiving a pass. While the forwards are forechecking, the defensemen stay just inside the attacking blue line. Once the forwards begin backchecking, the defensemen run back to the center line and turn quickly to face the attack. In their own end, the defensemen cover the puck carrier and the net. For example, if the puck is in the left corner, the left defenseman will check the puck carrier, while the right defenseman covers any opponent in front of the net.

Some important rules

Many of the rules in hockey, as in other games, are designed to make the game more interesting. Such rules require the players to maneuver with more skill and teamwork than if scoring goals were simply a free-for-all. Among the most important rules in ice hockey are those regarding "icing the puck," "advancing the puck," and "offside."

icing the puck

To ice the puck is to shoot it from behind the center red line all the way across the opposing team's goal line. It is not counted as icing if the puck goes into the goal (in which case the goal is allowed) or if it passes diagonally through the goal crease on its way across the line. The shot is also not counted as icing if an opponent touches or has a chance to play the puck before it crosses the line, or if the team of the player making the shot is short-handed. If icing is called, play is stopped and the puck faced off at one of the two face-off spots in the offending team's defending zone.

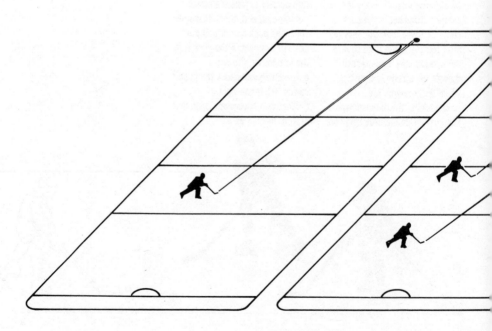

offside
A player is considered offside if, while his team is attacking, he crosses the defending team's blue line ahead of the puck. If the puck is passed from behind his own team's blue line, he is offside if he is beyond the red center line. It is the position of the player's skates, and not of his stick, that determines whether or not he is offside, and so long as one of his skates is inside the relevant line he is not counted offside. To avoid this infraction of the rules, practice cutting along the blue line, making sure one skate remains inside it. If offside is called, play is stopped, then resumed with a face-off either in the offender's defending zone or (if the offending team is short-handed) at the point where the pass was started.

advancing the puck
The puck must be advanced at all times. The team that has the puck must keep moving it toward the opposing goal, unless prevented by an opponent. This rule is designed to prevent a team from delaying the game. A minor penalty is imposed on a player (other than a goalkeeper) who deliberately holds the puck against the boards or goal, thus delaying the game – unless he is being checked by an opponent.

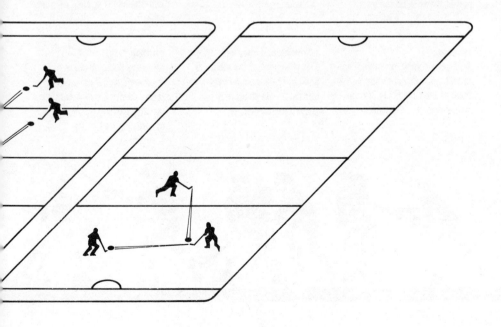

In ice hockey a certain amount of combat is part of the game. But there are certain moves that are against the rules. Some of the major fouls are illustrated below. Most carry either major or minor penalties, according to the circumstances. Obviously, fighting is against the rules, and a player deliberately injuring another may be removed for the remainder of the game.

cross checking
This is a check delivered with both hands on the stick and no part of the stick on the ice.

charging
To charge an opponent is to run into him or jump at him deliberately.

holding
As the name suggests, this foul consists of holding an opponent with the hands or stick or in any other way.

spearing
A player stabbing, or attempting to stab, an opponent with the point of the stick blade may be suspended from the game.

elbowing and kneeing
This is the use of the elbow or knee to check an opponent. Kicking an opponent may be given a match penalty.

slashing
Swinging the stick at an opponent, even if he is out of range, carries a minor or major penalty; slashing during a fight may result in a fine and suspension.

high sticking
This is the use of the stick, carried above shoulder level, against an opponent.

hooking
This foul consists of impeding or trying to impede an opponent with the stick.

butt-ending
To butt-end is to hit a player with the butt end of the stick with both hands on the stick and no part of it on the ice.

tripping
This is to cause an opponent to trip or fall by placing the stick or any part of one's body in his way. Tripping a player who has control of the puck and is in the attacking zone with no other opponent to pass than the goalkeeper results in a penalty shot for the non-offending team.

throwing a stick
If a defending player throws his stick at the puck in his defending zone and the attacking team fails to score a goal, a penalty shot is awarded.

Basically there are five kinds of penalty awarded against a team or a player:
Minor penalty – the offender is ruled off the ice for two minutes of actual playing time. No substitutes are allowed the team.
Major penalty – for a first offense the player is ruled off the ice for five minutes. No substitute is allowed , unless the goalie receives the penalty. Misconduct – awarded for abusive language to an official. The player is ruled off the ice for ten minutes, but the team is allowed a substitute. Match

1 cross checking. Fists are clenched and moved out from the chest.
2 charging. Clenched fists are rotated in front of the chest.

3 holding. One hand clasps the other wrist.
4 high sticking. Fists are clenched one above the other at shoulder height.

5 hooking. A tugging motion as if pulling something toward the stomach.

11 tripping. Right hand strikes right leg below knee.

12 spearing. Both hands are thrust out, making a jabbing motion, then dropped to the side.
13 clipping. Right hand strikes right leg behind knee.

14 roughing. With fist clenched, arm extends out in front of body.
15 interference. Arms crossed in front of chest, fists clenched.

– awarded against a player who deliberately attempts to injure an opponent. He is removed for the balance of the game, and his team must play shorthanded for 10 or 15 minutes.

Penalty shot – this is awarded when a player has been illegally impeded from behind while carrying the puck, provided no one apart from the goalie was between him and the goal. A player chosen by the captain may then play the puck down from the center face-off circle with no opposition except the goalie.

6 butt-ending. Forearms are moved back and forth, one over the other.

7 boarding. Clenched fist strikes opposite hand in front of chest.

8 kneeing. Palm slaps knee.

9 elbowing. Tapping either elbow with the opposite hand.

10 slashing. Edge of hand makes a chopping motion on forearm.

16 washout. Arms are swept sideways. Means "no goal" or, if made by linesman, "no icing" or "no offside."

17 icing. An arm raised overhead by referee or linesman indicates possible or completed icing, depending on position of official.

18 icing. Arms crossed over chest; stops play after icing has been established.

attacking zone	the area from the opposing team's blue line to the goal line.
backchecking	an attempt by forwards, while skating back to their own defensive zone, to regain the puck from the opposition.
backhand	a shot or pass taken on the left side by a right-handed player or on the right side by a left-handed player.
blind pass	passing the puck without looking.
breakaway	a puck carrier skating alone toward the goalkeeper with no opposing player between him and the net.
breakout	when the attacking team comes out of its defensive zone with the puck and starts up ice.
checking	defending against or guarding an opponent, especially with the aim of making him surrender the puck.
clearing the puck	keeping the puck away from one's own goal area.
cover	a defensive player staying close to an opponent in his own defensive zone so that he can't receive a pass.
cutting	crossing over one's skate stride while turning.
defensive zone	the area from a team's own goal line to their blue line.
deflect	to change the direction of the puck with the stick or with one's body.
deke	to fake a man out of position while carrying the puck.
feeding	passing the puck.
floater	an offensive player who slips into the center zone behind the attacking defensemen.
forechecking	checking an opponent in his defensive zone as he attempts to start a play.
freezing the puck	holding the puck against the boards with stick or skates in order to force a stoppage in play and a face-off.

get the jump	to get a fast start on an opponent.
hat trick	three or more goals scored by a single player in one game.
head-man	a quick pass by a defenseman to a forward breaking into center ice.
on the fly	changing players while the play is continuing.
penalty killer	a player whose job is to use up time while a teammate is serving a penalty.
playmaker	the player, usually the center, who sets up plays.
points	defenseman's position on the attacking blue line.
power play	the situation in which a team with a man advantage during a penalty sends five men into the short-handed team's defensive zone.
pulling the goalkeeper	replacing the goalkeeper with a forward. This move, which leaves the goal unguarded, is usually made as a last attempt to score a goal when the game is nearly over.
ragging	keeping possession of the puck by clever stick-handling.
rebound	a shot that bounces off the goalkeeper.
rush	an individual or combined attack by a team in possession of the puck.
scramble	several players from both sides battling for the puck in close-range action.
screen shot	a shot made through several players (opponents or teammates) and so unable to be seen by the goalie.
splitting the defense	the action of a puck carrier going through two defenseman.
trailer	a player who follows his attacking teammates, then moves into position to take a drop pass.

Bandy is related to ice hockey, but it differs in that it uses a ball, instead of a puck, and a curved stick. Also, the rink is larger — measuring at least 109 by 60yd(100 by 55m) — and 11 players from each team of 14 may be on the ice at one time.

starting play

A stroke-off from the center begins each 45-minute half and restarts play after a goal. The player stroking off plays the ball into the opponents' half and may not play it again until another player has touched it. Other players must stand at least 5½yd(5m) away from the ball at stroke-off. A stroke-in awarded to the opposition if the ball is played over the touchline. The ball is placed within 39in(1m) of where it crossed the line. Opponents must stand 5½yd(5m) away.

A face-off restarts play after an accidental stoppage. Two opposing players face each other at the point where the ball was when play stopped. They stand with their backs to their own goal lines, sticks parallel to and on either side of the ball. Other players stand at least 5½yd(5m) away.
The ball is played in at the referee's signal.

60yd
55m

109yd
100m

equipment

The stick is made of wood or similar material, without metal fittings or handstrap, and it may be up to 47in(120cm) long and 2.4in(6cm) wide. The ball is made of colored plastic or other approved material and weighs approximately 2oz(60g).

Players wear a helmet, a mouth protector, and padded gloves. The skates must have no sharp points or projections. Goalkeepers wear leg pads.

playing the ball

A player may: play the ball with his stick, kick the ball, and control the ball with his body, provided he has both skates on the ice.

tackling

A player may physically challenge an opponent who has the ball, or is challenging for it, but he may not kick, trip, push, grasp, or impede an opponent or his stick, or throw his stick at the ball.

goalkeepers

A goalkeeper does not use a stick. He may only be challenged when he has the ball or is impeding an opponent. Within his own penalty area he may use his skates or any part of his body to play the ball. After catching the ball he may carry it in one or both hands. He must release the ball as soon as possible and may only hold it for up to five seconds without moving.

scoring

A goal is scored when the ball crosses the line between the goalposts and under the crossbar. It cannot be scored directly from a stroke-off, stroke-in, face-off, or direct throw by the goalkeeper. The team that scores the greatest number of goals wins the game.

goal throw

A goal throw is awarded against an attacker who plays the ball over his opponents' goal line. The goal umpire rolls the ball along to the goalkeeper, who throws the ball into play.

corner stroke

A corner stroke is awarded against a defender who plays the ball over his own goal line. An opponent plays the ball in from within 39in(1m) of the nearest corner angle. He may not play the ball again until it has been touched by another player.

offside

A player is offside if, when the ball is played or touched by a teammate, he is in front of the ball within his opponents' half, unless there are at least two opponents nearer their goal line than he is.

As its name suggests this game is similar to ice hockey but is played on roller skates. A ball is used, instead of a puck, and the stick is curved.

The game originated in Britain around the beginning of the 20th century and is not played in many other countries. It's especially popular in Spain and Portugal.

the rink
It has a wooden, asphalt, or cement floor, coated with an abrasive powder to prevent its being slippery and is surrounded by an 8in(20cm) barrier. Dimensions of the rink vary from one country to another.
The rink is divided by a center line (a) on which is located the center spot (b) where the game begins with a strike-off. On the boundaries of the penalty areas (long rectangles) are several penalty spots (c), from which direct shots at the goal (d) are made, when awarded by the referee.

the team
Each team has five players including a goalkeeper. Five substitutes, including a substitute goalkeeper, are allowed. There must always be at least two players on the rink. Players can be substituted during the game; goalkeepers only during a stoppage.

officials
These include a referee who controls the game, assisted by: two goal judges, two timekeepers, and an official to keep a record of the time.

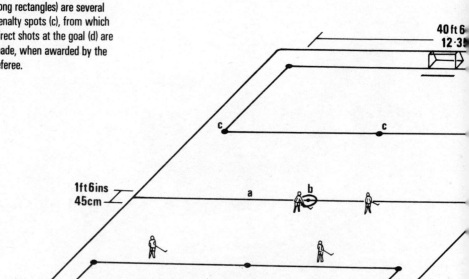

40 ft 6
12·3

1ft 6ins
45cm

equipment
The ball has a circumference of 9in(23cm) and must be of a color contrasting with the rink surface. The stick, which is made of wood, must be no longer than 3ft 9in(1.1m). The curved part is flattened on both sides.

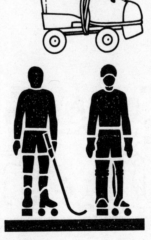

Skates are heavier than those used in artistic roller skating and have wider wheels and stronger toe stops.

18ft
5·50m

Players wear protective padding, including knee pads. Only goalkeepers may wear pads on their legs outside their clothing. They also wear helmets, face masks, and gloves.

duration
In international matches, a game consists of two periods, each of 20 minutes' playing time, separated by a three-minute interval. If both sides are equal at the end of the regular playing time, a three-minute rest is allowed, after which the teams begin a play-off, with the first team to score a goal being the winner.

starting play
The game begins with a strike-off
at the center spot. Two
opponents face each other with
their backs to their own goals.
Their sticks must be in front of
them and 9in(23cm) behind the
ball, which is placed on the spot.
At the referee's whistle they may
play the ball.

fouls
Players are not allowed to: play
the ball illegally; charge unfairly
(a); obstruct deliberately (b); fight,
kick, trip (c); throw, hold an
opponent or use the stick
against an opponent (d); tackle
unfairly.

playing the ball

A player may only play the ball with his stick, which may not be raised above his shoulders. He may stop the ball with his skates or any part of his body except his hands, provided it is not knocked forward to his team's advantage.

When shooting, a player may hit the ball with the flat part of the blade, not with the sharp edge (chopping).

The ball must not rise above 5ft (1.5m) unless it ricochets off two sticks outside the penalty area. The goalkeeper is allowed to play the ball within his penalty area with any part of his body, including his hands, but he must not deliberately trap the ball.

A goal is scored when the entire ball crosses the line between the goal posts.

penalties

An indirect frank hit – or free hit –may be awarded to the opponents of a team committing a foul. The ball is stationary for the hit, and opponents must be at least 9ft(2.7m) away. The player taking the hit may not play the ball again until it has been touched by another player. A goal may not be scored direct from an indirect frank hit.

A direct frank hit is awarded for more serious fouls. All players, except the one taking the hit and the goalkeeper, stand 15ft(4.6m) behind the ball; they must not move until the ball is played. The goalkeeper must be behind the crease line, but his stick may be in front of it. A goal may be scored direct, but a direct shot is not necessary.

A penalty shot is a direct shot from a penalty spot, and is awarded for serious infringements of rules within the penalty area. All players, except the one taking the shot and the goalkeeper, must be behind the center line. The goalkeeper must be behind the crease line. No player may move until the ball is played. The striker may not play the ball again unless it has hit the goalkeeper or the outside of the goal.

A player committing a foul may be sent off for any period up to 5 minutes' playing time, or for the rest of the game. He cannot be replaced by a substitute. For a second offense, a player must be sent off for the rest of the match.

out of play

If the ball is played out of the rink, the opposition is awarded an indirect free hit. It is taken 2½ft (76cm) from where the ball crossed the barrier.

A strike-off is awarded: if the ball ricochets off two sticks; if it was deliberately played to obtain a free hit; or if the referee is uncertain which team last played the ball.

Skateboarding

A skateboarder demonstrates perfect control as he climbs a wall on his board.

This exhilarating new sport has features in common with both roller skating and surfing. Primitive kinds of skateboard were constructed by children in the early part of this century, using old roller skate wheels and orange crates. But the sport really took off only a few years ago, when surfers discovered that they could achieve some of the thrills of riding the waves by zooming over the pavement on a small version of a surfboard equipped with wheels.

Protective clothing will minimize the chance of an injury. A lightweight helmet, elbow and knee pads (which can be homemade from towelling), and thick gloves are recommended. Long pants will protect the skin on your legs, and sneakers will help keep you from slipping. For added safety cover the top of the skateboard—the deck—with some grip tape.

Skateboards come in a variety of shapes, sizes, and materials. The beginner should choose a board with a flexible deck that springs quickly back into shape. The trucks—the metal parts that hold the wheels on the deck—should be of the double action type, which permits you to steer the board, and the wheels should be of urethane.

Executing the slalom in a skateboard competition.

As in any other sport, you must learn the basics of skateboarding before you attempt any of the spectacular tricks that make it so exciting. First learn how to get on and off the board, how to balance on it and steer it, and how to protect yourself during a fall. Then you can advance to more ambitious maneuvers.

Begin on a flat surface and learn the basic position. Place one foot over the front axle, at a slight angle to the length of the board. Then place the other foot over the rear axle, at a slightly greater angle. When both feet are on the board, you may want to turn the front foot parallel to the rear one.

To build up speed on a flat surface, you must learn to scoot, or shunt. Start with the front foot on the board, as usual. Push off with the other foot, as you would on a scooter. For more speed push again as often as necessary. Between pushes place the foot on the rear of the board as already described.

To get off the board when it is moving, step off in the direction of travel and grasp the skateboard as shown.

A flat surface is essential when you're just getting used to your skateboard. You can propel yourself over it by scooting. A sloping surface gives you momentum so that you can perform various tricks on the board. On a curved surface the advanced skateboarder can defy gravity and literally climb the walls on his board.

To reduce the chance of injury in a fall, try to break the impact of the fall by rolling over, with your head tucked in and your body relaxed.

If you keep your weight evenly balanced on the board, so that it is parallel to the surface on which you're skating, you'll move forward in a straight line. To move in a curve, to the left or to the right, you must adjust your balance by leaning either backward on your heels or forward on your toes. If most of your weight is on the left side of the board, it will move toward the left; if most of it is on the right side of the board, the board will move toward the right. These turns are only gradual ones; for sharper steering you must master the kick turn.

crouching
This is a simple but pleasurable maneuver that naturally increases your speed because in this position you present less resistance to the wind.

handstand
First crouch and grip the ends of the board. Kick up your legs, at the same time locking your elbows. When you come down, try to land with your feet pointing forward so that you can run along and gradually lose your momentum.

two-board wheelie
This requires expert balance on the front or back axles of two boards. Start by learning how to balance this way on one board before trying the two-board version.

crouching daffy
This is an advanced version of the two-board wheelie in which the front foot does a tail (back) wheelie while the rear foot does a nose (front) wheelie.

bunny hop
Crouch down as for a handstand and jump, holding onto the skateboard.

kick turn

Try this first on a static board. Move the rear foot back to the tail of the board, angling it more sharply than in the basic position shown earlier. Shift nearly all your weight to the rear foot so that the front wheels rise off the ground. Now – depending on the direction you want to turn –

either pull the front foot back or push it forward. The impetus for the turn comes from twisting the hips, while the front foot guides the board.

back-boarding

Sit on the board with your bottom just behind the front axle and stretch your arms and legs out as shown. Use your stomach muscles to control your balance. Don't try to get off the skateboard until it comes to a stop.

royal Christie

This is a difficult maneuver. Start by moving your front leg – for example, the left one – to the front of the board and bringing your right arm forward so that both arms are across the direction of travel. Crouch down, at the same time bringing the right leg out at about a 30-40° angle, keeping the knee straight.

catamaran

This requires teamwork but is relatively safe and simple. The two skaters sit facing each other and holding hands with their feet on each others' boards. To turn left, the partner on the left leans backward; to turn right the one on the right leans backward.

Skateboarding down an inclined plane isn't just a simple matter of rolling along and letting gravity take over. You've got to learn how to control your speed by steering the board across the line of travel and how to achieve greater speed when you need it.

slalom

This race is similar to the ski slalom. Markers (which may be tin cans) are placed in a curved line and skaters required to weave back and forth around them. The race begins with a straight run up to the second starting line, after which the feet must not touch the ground. The swerving movements must be only just wide enough to clear the markers — which are placed between 4 and 8ft(1.2 and 2.4m) apart — so as not to delay your progress unnecessarily. An expert slalom racer leans over the marker as he goes around it, straightens up as he approaches the next, then leans in the other direction as he goes around the next.

cranking

This is the technique of building speed in a straight race by moving up and down from a high to a low crouch and back.

traversing and wedeling
These terms, taken from skiing, refer to sideways motions that keep you from accelerating too fast. For traversing you need a fairly wide slope that will enable you to make wide turns,

steering the board as explained earlier. Wedeling is the technique of moving across the line of travel in very quick sharp curves. By turning slightly uphill you can further check your speed and brake to a stop.

Toe-tapping is another way of coming to a stop. Lift the rear foot off the board and tap the ground at intervals. Don't try this if you're moving very fast.

If you're at all ambitious about skating — that is, if you want to do more than just glide around the rink in a leisurely fashion — you'll find that you must be fit. The exercise you get while skating should be supplemented by exercise off the ice. That way, you can concentrate on perfecting the specific skills you need — jumping a double Axel, or executing a flip shot — without having to worry about running out of wind or going wobbly in the knees.

Probably the most useful exercise for skaters — whether they're figure skaters, speed skaters, or hockey players — is jogging. This will help you to develop stamina. If you find it boring, try jogging with a friend.

for figure skaters
Both dancing and gymnastics offer good opportunities for increasing your poise and muscular control. A little ballet – particularly the warming-up exercises – can be helpful. Try some pliés. Stand with one hand holding onto some steady piece of furniture (in a ballet class you would have a barre) and the other hand held out to the side. Place your feet about one foot-length apart, toes turned out as far as possible. Keeping your back straight and your seat tucked in, bend your knees until your thighs are parallel to the floor. Don't lift your heels or let your ankles roll forward. Slowly rise to a standing position. Repeat.

There are many gymnastic movements that relate to figure skating. The split leap shown here is an obvious example. Notice how the head is kept well up and the arms out to the side throughout the jump.

Simply walking with a book on your head will help you to gain poise. Use your arms for balance.

Once you've mastered walking with the book on your head, see if you can crouch without dropping it.

Grands battements are another good warming-up step. Hold onto the piece of furniture with your left hand and hold your right arm out to the side. Place your right heel at your left toe, with both feet turned out as far as possible. Now raise your right leg straight up and forward, keeping the knee straight and pointing the toe hard. Bring the leg down again quickly. Only the working leg should move during the battement; the rest of the body remains still. Next, kick the leg out to the side and bring it down behind the left foot, right toe to left heel. Finally, raise it behind and bring it back into position. Repeat this exercise several times with the right leg, then turn and repeat it using the left leg.

for hockey skaters

Plenty of jogging will help you keep in shape. For a change of pace, try cycling. Other sports that involve running – such as tennis, soccer, and field hockey – provide good exercise.

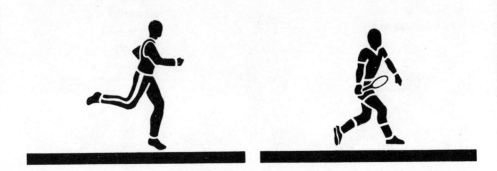

160